Leading the Dream!

The Journey of a Successful Charter School

By Debo Powers

John - For all of
Thanks for all of
your help & support
over the years.

Debo

First Edition 2014

ISBN-13: 978-1502981158

ISBN-10: 1502981157

Arts and Sciences

*Dedicated to the past, present, and future
students, teachers, parents, staff, and board members
of the School of Arts and Sciences....
and the founders who had the vision to get things started.*

Table of Contents

Preface

From an early age, I believed that one person could make a difference. Growing up as a white child in the South during the Civil Rights Movement, I saw people risking everything to make the society in which I lived a better place. I believed that I could do that too. Throughout my youth, I focused on places where things needed to be improved and tried to make a difference in whatever way I could.

I became interested in history and politics and majored in those subjects in college. As a young person, changing the world seemed not only possible, but necessary. When I looked for a career, I chose teaching because teachers have the opportunity to change lives every day.

My teaching career started in a rural county outside of Tallahassee, Florida. The school system was underfunded with buildings, books, and teaching materials in poor condition. Most of my middle school students were black and economically deprived and were reading far below their grade level. Due to my classroom situation where the textbooks were outdated and above the reading level of my students, I created my own thematic lessons with an emphasis on building self-esteem and teaching black history. This was my first opportunity to think about and create something different than a textbook-driven curriculum.

After my first three years of teaching in a rural county, I obtained a teaching position in Tallahassee in one of the most innovative public high schools in the nation where I taught for the next seventeen years. It was there that I became inspired by the idea of creating schools where everyone was respected fully and where all students could flourish regardless of their learning style or background.

As a teacher and a mother, I participated in the growing alternative school movement in Tallahassee. It was this passion for educational change that kept me living and working in Tallahassee when I was drawn to the Northern Rockies where I spent summers. I had discovered the place of my heart while backpacking in Glacier National Park in 1979. Every summer afterwards, I returned to this remote paradise for "re-charging time" throughout my education career. It was my time to think and dream and reconnect with myself before the next busy school year.

Sometimes someone says something to you and it changes your life forever. That's what happened to me in the spring of 1998 when my friend Terry said: "There is a group of educational reformers that plans to open a charter school and they're looking for a principal." I was intrigued because I had been pondering where one could make the most impact in changing education for the better. At that time I was a classroom teacher in a very innovative public high school, but I was searching for a bigger leadership role in transforming education. Although I had not heard about this new charter school, I asked Terry for a copy of the charter application.

Until then, I hardly knew what a charter school was and had no idea what the organizers of this proposed school had in mind. However, while reading the charter application, my heart rate quickened at the description of the school as envisioned in the document. My imagination was fueled by the possibility of creating a new public school with a thematic, hands-on, project-based curriculum that would be different from traditional public schools and could serve as a model for change. In my heart, I knew that this was the school for me. In addition, I saw this project as a way to put my ideas about collaborative leadership into practice. At the time, I had no idea how hard I would work, how much I would learn, or how my own life would change as a result of my decision to lead this project.

My decision to spearhead this project began an adventure into the charter school world that was still new and relatively unexplored territory in 1998. After thirteen years at the helm of this project, I decided to write this book in order to share the story of our challenges and successes and the philosophy behind what we accomplished.

My hope is that this book will inspire people with innovative ideas to create the school of their dreams. Anyone who starts down this path will encounter obstacles and challenges as we did, but the result may be better than you have been able to imagine. If we could do it, so could you.

Introduction

Unlike Karl Weber's pro-charter school book *Waiting for 'Superman'* (Public Affairs, 2010) that criticizes district-run public schools and asserts that public charter schools are the answer, this book does neither. Rather, this book is the story of one charter school's journey from a dream to greatness, a story of struggle and hard work and following a vision.

This book is written in three sections.

Section I is the story of the School of Arts and Sciences in Tallahassee, Florida. The story is told through the lens of a principal who had to weather many attacks while running an award-winning charter school. Although the story is told from my perspective as the principal, this is not just my personal memoir. It is the story of how a small group of dedicated educators and parents created a school from nothing but dreams and hard work; a school that would be recognized by the US Department of Education as one of the top eight charter schools in the nation just five years after its doors opened. This is a story of commitment, passion, and persistence—a real labor of love—that continues to enrich the lives of young people, teachers, and parents who have had the good fortune to be a part of it.

Section II of this book describes the educational philosophy of our school and how that philosophy is put into practice every day at the School of Arts and Sciences. Starting with the foundation of a respectful learning environment, it details the implementation of our philosophy in the day-to-day workings of the classrooms, the finances, and the organizational structure. This section will be helpful for those interested in creating a school with a similar philosophy.

Many lessons were learned in the course of creating and operating an innovative charter school. Some of those lessons are discussed in Section III of this book. Some things in this section will be helpful for those developing any kind of collaborative organizational structure, charter school or otherwise. The last chapter spells out some of my personal views on the charter school movement after being intimately involved in it for more than a decade.

Background on Charter Schools

When I first heard about charter schools, I had no idea what they were. I had many misconceptions, as is common among the general population. Before embarking on this story, we should clear up some of the usual misunderstandings.

Misconception #1. Charter schools take money away from public schools. Charter schools are PUBLIC SCHOOLS. Charter schools do not take money away from public schools because they <u>are part of the public school system</u>. The difference is that charter schools can operate (somewhat) outside of the traditional school district, and because of this they have the opportunity to be more flexible and innovative. The charter school legislation empowers teachers and parents to create the school of their dreams rather than just accept what is available.

Misconception #2. Charter schools are not held accountable. Those who wish to start a charter school must submit an application to a state-approved authorizer (in Florida, the local school district) that details the vision, curriculum design, organization, and budget for the proposed school. This application is approved before opening. Those who operate charter schools are held to a very high standard of accountability that is more than just standardized test scores. If a charter school has a good model, the students are successful, and the funds are managed responsibly, then the school can continue to provide an educational program. If not, the school can be closed down. In the state of Florida, most charter schools receive their approval to operate from the district school board who extends or terminates the charter after certain specified periods of time. If the school's charter is denied or the school is terminated after being in operation, they can appeal the decision to the Charter School Appeals Commission.

Misconception #3. Charter schools take all of the brightest and best students. Charter schools are open to all students. Students apply to attend a charter school. If more students apply than openings available, there is a random lottery which assures that everyone has the chance to attend. If a student's name is drawn in the lottery, they can enroll in the school.

Misconception #4. All charter schools are alike. There are as many different types of charter schools as there are ideas about education. Each one has its own philosophy of education and methods for teaching and helping young people excel. Some charter schools serve a small number of students while others have huge student enrollment. Charter school management is structured in different ways. Some charter schools are independent, while others operate with the help of a management company.

The School of Arts and Sciences is a kindergarten through eighth grade charter school serving 270 students with an innovative, hands-on curriculum and a waiting list more than three times the student population. The school operates independently without a management company but with a very active board of directors. This is our story.

To facilitate individual educational ownership and responsible lifelong learning through interdisciplinary approaches to arts and sciences in a safe and nurturing environment.

Mission Statement for School of Arts and Sciences

Good charter schools are mission-driven. Every step of the way, through every challenging obstacle, school leaders must use the mission as a flashlight to illuminate where the path leads.
Debo Powers

Section I: The Story

Chapter 1: The Dreaming Years 1996-1999

A charter school starts with a dream...or it should. It should not just be a cookie-cutter replica of what already exists everywhere. It should be innovative and offer something different. It should excite the imagination of educators and parents and bring out their creative energy.

We had grand dreams about how our school would be innovative. We wanted to be different from traditional public schools. A school with a traditional format is characterized by classrooms that are set up with individual desks in rows with students facing a teacher, the giver of all knowledge. The classroom is teacher-centered; the teacher presents the information and directs everything. Students march through textbooks and all are given the same assignments, such as answering the questions at the end of each chapter. All of the students in the classroom are doing the same thing at the same time, and they are graded against each other. Finally, tests are given to make sure that they have mastered the material. The teacher typically teaches to the middle range in the classroom, leaving the struggling students feeling stupid and the more advanced students feeling bored. While there is some variation from this norm and heightened awareness regarding differentiated instruction, the above description applies to most classrooms in this country.

We wanted something different for the students than the typical "factory model" of education. Rather than sit at their desks all day and be passive learners, we envisioned a school where the students could be actively engaged in their learning. We didn't want to produce young people who would do only what they are told to do; we wanted students to think critically, analyze, research, use their creativity, produce projects, and present what they had learned to their peers. We concluded that our society needs thinkers and leaders who can find new ways of doing things, collaborate well with others, speak with confidence in public, and share their ideas. We knew as educators that young people tend to learn best in an environment where they could practice these skills and develop them. They would not be able to do this sitting all day at desks being passive learners. We also knew that in order to accomplish these goals, students needed to be able to work cooperatively and discuss with each other what they were learning.

Turning this dream into reality would require a lot of effort from a great many people. A charter school should evolve because a person or a group of people wants something different than what is available. Our dream of having a charter school did not spring from nowhere. Our dream had deep roots in the culture of Tallahassee, Florida where many people had been dreaming about different ways to educate their children for some time.

Referred to as "The Berkeley of the South" in the late sixties, Tallahassee has been a center of progressive thinking for many decades. Participation in the various member owned co-operatives (both stores and neighborhoods) has given many Tallahassee residents places to learn how to organize and develop self-reliance from the dominate culture. Beginning with the Grassroots Free School founded by Pat Seery in the sixties, Tallahassee has a long history of alternative schools. Other private elementary/middle schools followed in their footsteps. Susan Smith started Magnolia School (1985), Drs. Carolyn and Gerry Schluck started the Schluck School (1988), Irwin Freidman started Full Flower School (1989), and Betsey and Tony Brown, along with a core group of teachers, started Cornerstone School (2000). All of these schools were based on models that utilized "hands-on" learning.

Most of the early alternative schools in Tallahassee have been private schools. However, in the mid-seventies, Joel Dawson and other educational pioneers started the Alternative Learning Center that later became the School for Applied Individualized Learning (SAIL) High School under the leadership of Rosanne Wood. Within the district school system, SAIL was a small high school that offered an innovative curriculum aimed at students who were not interested, or not successful, in the traditional setting of high school. As such, it had to fight for its existence every year for the first decade at the Leon County School Board meetings packed with SAIL parents who wanted this alternative for their kids. Thanks to the SAIL parents and teachers and the forward-thinking school board members and superintendents who supported it, this school has not only survived, but has thrived as one of the highest performing high schools in the district despite serving students who march to the beat of a different drummer.

Another public alternative was founded in the late 1970s and was called the Hartsfield Program. This innovative program operated within a traditional elementary school as a "school within a school," and used the instructional methods of the British Infant System. This approach utilizes a multi-age, child-centered classroom with the teacher operating as a facilitator of hands-on learning. Dr. Carolyn Schluck, from the Education Department at Florida State University, was instrumental in advocating for this program and training the teachers. However, due to dissent from other teachers at the school and lack of support at the district level, it was abandoned. In response, Dr. Schluck started the Schluck School based on the same philosophy as the Hartsfield Program.

I was a part of this Tallahassee alternative school movement having taught at SAIL High School beginning in 1978. In addition, my daughter attended Full Flower School from kindergarten through eighth grade followed by SAIL for high school. One of the reasons that I stayed in Tallahassee was because it was a cauldron of progressive ideas about education, and educational change was my passion.

All of the alternative schools mentioned above pioneered a new type of learning program that offered young people the opportunity to create and explore through hands-on learning. These were programs where students were active learners rather than sitting at desks all day. The problem was that with the exception of SAIL High School and the Hartsfield Program, all of them were private schools, and because parents had to pay tuition, these schools found it difficult to attract a diverse student population. Parents who sent their children to these private schools tended to be white, middle class, and liberal thinkers. However, the work that they did paved the way for the School of Arts and Sciences. There were so many people searching for an alternative to traditional education in Tallahassee that there was a "brain bank" of philosophy and experience. The School of Arts and Sciences stands on the shoulders of these early pioneers.

This desire for alternative schools did not exist because there were only underperforming schools in our community. To the contrary, the Leon County School District has always been a high-performing district in the state of Florida. However, the district schools tend to be set up in traditional ways. It was opposition to these traditional methods that resulted in the proliferation of alternative schools (both public and private) in Tallahassee for more than thirty years.

and solved problems in the school or community. These service projects would also build a sense of social responsibility.

5. **Teaching Foreign Languages**

   Students would learn foreign languages with an emphasis on Spanish. The founders believed that learning other languages is important in a multicultural world.

6. **Big Buddy/Little Buddy Classrooms**

   Classrooms with older students would work with classrooms with younger students so that students had "big buddies" and "little buddies" to enhance the learning process. Among other things, the founders envisioned younger students reading to older students and vice versa.

7. **Experiential Learning and Construction Projects**

   Hands-on learning would be more prevalent than passive learning in the classrooms. In other words, textbooks would not drive the instruction. The founders believed that learning occurs most readily when people gain knowledge by experience and see how that knowledge can be applied in the world. They envisioned students who would learn by doing through making books, exploring the natural environment, and designing and constructing models, dioramas, and projects.

8. **Serve Grades Kindergarten through Twelve**

The founders envisioned a school that would serve kindergarten through twelfth grade students and have an enrollment of 325 students.

The founders also envisioned a school with a nurturing, respectful environment where students would learn to collaborate as they developed into leaders and community builders. The school would be small enough to facilitate connections between people, ensuring a family atmosphere. Although the new charter school would need to be bigger than the private alternative schools in Tallahassee for budgetary reasons, the founders wanted to keep the school as small as possible in order to retain its philosophy and character.

After many meetings, long discussions, and numerous revisions, the charter application was finally completed and submitted to the Leon County School Board in 1997. Although many people worked on the charter along the way, the group had dwindled by the time the charter application was submitted. The charter listed only five people as the founders. Two were university professors, Dr. Carolyn Schluck and Dr. Gerry Schluck, who had started and operated a private school called the Schluck School. Dr. Carolyn Schluck, from the Education Department at Florida State University, had also trained teachers in the Hartsfield Program discussed earlier in this chapter. Dr. Roger Pinholster was a district assistant principal on track to become a district principal. There were two teachers: Mary Markin and Maureen Yoder.

The founders became the core of the first board of directors with the exception of Maureen, who was promised a teaching position at the new school. Mary Markin became the board chair. In addition, two involved parents were added to the first board.

After being submitted to the Leon County School Board, the charter was initially denied because it did not include achievement goals based on standardized testing. The new board of directors revised the charter application, re-submitted it, and won approval by the school board in April 1998. The school was granted a three-year charter and was expected to open in August of that year.

After the approval of the charter application, the board began to hold public meetings on Thursday nights in the Education Building of the First Presbyterian Church. These meetings were well attended by parents who were enthusiastic about the plans for a new public charter school. Many of them had been taxing their family budgets on private schooling and were excited about a small public school that offered a progressive philosophy. Discussions about school logistics, including transportation and lunches, occurred at these meetings and involved parents in designing the school. In addition, many fundraisers were organized and managed by parent committees. A celebration picnic was held in A.J. Henry Park in early May to bring families and board members together. By May, the proposed school already had almost full enrollment and a waiting list in some grades. Parents also organized swimming and skating parties so that the middle school students could get to know each other.

The new board discussed who should be the "principal teacher" of the new school. The board chair was very interested in the job, but was nearing retirement age and her husband asked that she not take on this new responsibility. Dr. Pinholster, the district assistant principal on the board, was another possibility, but he decided to stay with the district. The board discussed what they were looking for in a principal teacher and decided to advertise in the newspaper.

With an approved charter, the search was on to find a business manager, a principal teacher, and a school site. Fortunately, John Smith, a friend of the board chair, agreed to become the business manager. John was retired from the banking business and very interested in the charter school concept. He agreed to use his financial expertise to see that this school was successful. Even better, he was willing to work during the organizational stage without a salary until the school was opened.

The biggest problem facing the board was the school's location. The board had to find a building that would meet state standards for a public school, but still be affordable. They looked at hundreds of buildings. They were negotiating a lease on a building in downtown Tallahassee near the Florida Department of Education when I was hired as the principal. Many people wonder how a charter school can be approved without a location. The reason for this is that a group cannot expend resources on leasing or purchasing property unless they know for sure that the charter has been approved. Before the days of federal start-up grants, groups had to negotiate bank loans for their early expenses. While everyone donated their time, money had to be found for a building...and buildings were not cheap.

Despite the fact that the location was still in question, the founding board knew that they needed to hire a school leader to pull everything together. The advertised salary for the principal teacher was below the beginning salary for a district principal. The board's idea was that the principal teacher would be a teacher who also handled the administrative details. Not many principals wanted to leave their better-paying jobs to accept responsibility for turning a dream into a school, especially if they were expected to teach as well as lead. In addition, there would be no salary for the principal teacher until the school opened. It was lucky for me that they advertised this position as a "principal teacher" because many qualified people didn't take a second look.

*****

At this point in my life, I was an enthusiastic 47 year old woman who had the knowledge that comes from having lived almost a half century while still energized by the idealism of youth. My daughter, Emma, was in the seventh grade and her life was filled with activities and friends. After being a stay-at-home mom for several years, I had worked part-time as a classroom teacher during Emma's preschool and elementary years in order to have more time for her. Now that she was older, I had the freedom to explore my own dreams.

During the ten years when I worked as a part-time high school social studies teacher (which followed ten years as a full-time teacher), I had a small educational consulting business and led workshops for classroom teachers throughout the state of Florida. I was able to manage the time away from Emma because her father and I had a shared custody agreement and she lived with him half of the time. Although my consulting business was sporadic and usually occurred during teacher planning days or summer vacation, it fulfilled me in many ways because I enjoyed working with teachers who were eager for new ideas. In addition, I felt like I was making a difference in some small way to the classrooms of the teachers whom I taught. However, I soon tired of sleeping in motels and eating in restaurants and I began to wonder what real impact my workshops had without sustained contact with these teachers. I started pondering where the critical points that a person might be able to bring about change in the educational system were. I was looking for something more than teaching, something that would challenge me in a big way, something that would shake my complacency and scare me because of the enormity of the task.

I had thought about running for the district school board. I made an appointment with a local school board member whom I respected. When we met, we discussed her job responsibilities, the challenges, and the logistics of running for election. I had often dreamed about going into politics as an avenue for changing society. The idea of running for the school board thrilled me, but my partner was dead set against it. He did not want the scrutiny and nastiness that a political life often brings. Without having support from home, I decided to set that idea aside.

Next, I pursued a position that entailed periodic traveling throughout the world leading workshops on educational change. I was one of four people who were considered for this position in an international organization that I had been involved in for almost 20 years. I wanted that position badly, but realized that the leader of this organization wanted someone from outside the United States. I decided to put the organization ahead of my own desires and place my support behind one of the other four finalists, a dear friend who was an educational change leader in Trinidad. She got the job. I kept looking. I knew that my leadership position was out there somewhere.

After reading the charter application for the School of Arts and Sciences, I was excited about the vision for the school. After teaching for twenty years, the idea of a whole school that was focused on hands-on learning was exciting to me. With no previous experience in school administration and without the proper degree, I set my sights on getting the job of principal for the new charter school. I worked hard on a portfolio that spelled out my qualifications, experience, and philosophy of education. While teaching at SAIL High School, I had played a major part in the development of that innovative program and this experience was one of my qualifications that most interested the board. My experience at SAIL combined with my obvious passion for educational change, made me an attractive candidate. I also had leadership experience in various organizations where I had worked with all kinds of people and had led workshops in educational change and leadership development. I knew how to communicate information with enthusiasm, had a positive outlook, and an ability to work hard and commit myself to a project. I really wanted this job. Although I am an outdoors woman rather than a "girly girl," I bought a new professional-looking outfit for my interview, had my hair styled, wore make-up, and manicured my nails. I even looked like a principal!

I met the board for the first time around the dining room table in Julie Sullivan's home on June 3, 1998. Lyn Kittle was there as a parent representative to the board. The interview was conducted in a very professional, yet relaxed, way. The tone of the meeting was one of positive expectation and I felt confident about myself and the information that I gave them. During this two-hour interview, I presented my qualifications and my vision for the school. Many questions were asked and answered. One of the many important topics that we discussed was the role of the principal teacher. From my experience watching and supporting Rosanne Wood as the principal at SAIL High School, I was concerned that being the principal was more than a full-time job by itself. There would be no time for a teaching schedule in addition to the huge role and responsibilities of being the school leader. I told them that if they wanted a principal, I was the person for the job. If they expected someone who would be both a principal and a classroom teacher, they should choose someone else.

I had no sooner changed my clothes at home after the interview than I received a call offering me the job. I was thrilled...and scared. I had been searching for a position of leadership where I could make a difference in the world and this opportunity filled me with hope. However, I also knew that I was entering new territory and that I would inevitably make lots of mistakes as I figured things out. The fact of the matter is that I had no idea what I was getting into. It is hard to imagine, for anyone who hasn't done it, what it is like to start a school from scratch, to take a dream and make it a reality. In my naïve innocence, I was determined to make this happen. The words of Georgia O'Keeffe ran continuously through my mind and became my mantra: "I've been absolutely terrified every moment of my life, and I've never let it keep me from doing a single thing I wanted to do." Luckily, I had that idealism and determination or I might not have accepted the position at all.

Opening this school was the biggest challenge of my life. There were so many people to work with and they each had their own mental picture about what the school would be like. Just coordinating all of those visions was a huge task, and on top of that, there were a lot of logistical details including hiring teachers, furnishing classrooms, and student transportation. The list seemed endless. I started working as hard as I could to handle all those details and didn't stop for thirteen years. Even though the charter application used the term principal teacher, from the beginning I referred to myself as the principal and did not have a teaching schedule.

*****

The first thing that I did as the new principal was to walk through the downtown building that the board had decided would be the school's location. When I first saw the building from the outside, I thought that it looked like the place where Dr. Martin Luther King Jr. had been assassinated. It was a stark, two story building that had once been a motel with an open balcony/walkway on both levels with doors opening into the interior. The building had been renovated to accommodate some state government offices and many of the original interior walls had been removed to create suites of cubicles for workers. At this time, the building was empty and the suites could easily be transformed into large classrooms. Outside, the building had a paved parking lot and no green space for playground areas. There was a small city "park" a block away that was little more than a vacant lot with some grass and a few trees that board members optimistically thought could be developed as a play area for students. Although not an ideal school property, the building was close to museums, galleries, and the state capitol that could be visited for educational field trips. We were excited about being downtown and the possibilities of turning this old building into our dream school.

Shortly after being hired as the principal, I attended the statewide charter school conference with board chair, Mary Markin. As we drove down to Orlando for the conference, we had the opportunity to get to know each other better. The charter school movement was in its first years and there was a tone of high excitement and expectation at the conference. These were the days when the charismatic Tracey Bailey led the School Choice Office at the Florida Department of Education. His energy and optimism permeated the entire conference. Everyone there had just opened a charter school or was planning to do so in the next year. I got the sense that I was with a group of people who really believed that they could change the world by changing education. Although I did not know anyone there, I spent a lot of time talking to people in order to discover what was driving them and it seemed to me that there were three very different groups of educators at the conference who had distinctively different goals for starting a charter school.

One prominent group at the conference was African American educators who wanted to start schools that were more responsive to the needs of African American young people than the traditional schools. Another group was the people who had ideological or religious reasons for supporting charter schools. Some of them believed that public education had not worked and were in favor of the privatization of education.

They saw charter schools as a step in that direction. Some had left the public schools to homeschool their children because they did not approve of the ideas to which their children were exposed in public schools, but now wanted them in a school that would be more consistent with their ideals. The third group, to which I belonged, considered themselves educational reformers who were primarily interested in starting charter schools that had an innovative curriculum not offered in the public schools. It was interesting to me that people were drawn to charter schools for such different reasons and that this movement offered the chance to build coalitions among people who had very different political beliefs.

Some people are motivated to start charter schools because they have school-age children and they want something better for them than what is offered in traditional public education. Since my daughter was already attending an innovative private school and had the option of attending an innovative public high school in a few years, my motivation did not come from my parenting role. Rather, it came from my desire for world change and my belief that one person can make a difference. I generally opt for hopefulness and activism rather than despair when I contemplate the state of the world.

After returning from the conference inspired and ready to work, there was much to be done. Our plan was to open the school in August, just two months after I was hired. While many new charter schools have to do a lot of advertising for student enrollment, we did not have that problem. Word of our proposed school had spread like wildfire through our community and parents were hungry for an innovative public school for their children. We had a waiting list of more students than we had room for and their parents were very involved. Throughout the summer, fifty to one hundred parents met every week to work on school logistics and ask questions. We listened to parent input about everything from school lunches to discipline.

At this same time, the board and I were focused on two main tasks: securing a building (the board's job) and hiring and training the teachers (the principal's job). Every other day or so, I received a call from a board member to look at another possible site since we did not have a signed contract on the downtown site. Simultaneously, I was advertising for teachers.

We used a committee interview process for hiring teachers and I made the final decisions after receiving feedback from the committee. The board chair told me that it was important that I do the final hiring so that the teachers would see me as their leader and start to feel loyal to me. This was a successful idea with one exception. The one teacher who I didn't hire was the founder who had been promised a teaching position by the other founders before I was hired. I was told that she automatically had a job and did not have to go through the interview process. My relationship with this teacher was somewhat problematic throughout my thirteen years with the school. Many times I recalled the words of the first board chair about loyalty because that was one element that seemed to be missing in our relationship. She was one of my biggest critics on the staff and I think that the roots of our issues with each other stem back to this early situation--she was a founder and she never seemed to happily accept that I was the school leader. I continued to reinstate her each year because of her commitment to the school, but we struggled with our relationship. I would encourage founding boards to avoid putting principals in this situation.

After the twelve teachers were hired, we began training in multi-age, thematic instruction. Dr. Carolyn Schluck, a founder and board member, did a large part of the training. There was tension between the board chair and Dr. Schluck concerning Dr. Schluck's involvement in the teacher training. This was the first struggle to differentiate the roles of the board and the staff in the operation of the school. Dr. Schluck thought that as the most knowledgeable person on multi-age thematic instruction, she should be training the teachers. Others on the board, such as the chair, thought that a board member should not be so closely involved in the operation of the school. It was suggested that if she wanted to train the teachers, Dr. Schluck should resign from the board. In order to smooth the controversy, I proposed a policy which stated that when volunteering at the school, a board member would be under the direction and supervision of the school staff. When I made this proposal, many of the board members looked at me like I was nuts. I think that they were wondering if this new, inexperienced principal could handle this situation.

However, they approved the policy and Dr. Schluck continued to be involved in teacher training. This put me in the role of supervising Dr. Schluck, which unfortunately led to some tension between us at times.

Although the teachers were grateful for Dr. Schluck's insights and knowledge, they found it difficult to stay focused on her presentations. They complained to me and I did my best to help Dr. Schluck organize her workshops in a way that would meet the teachers' needs. It was definitely uncomfortable to be in the middle of this conflict, but it was worth the effort to get these important ideas and methods into teachers' toolboxes. These ideas included how to develop interdisciplinary themes that encompassed reading, writing, science, social studies, and math. Dr. Schluck taught the teachers how to help students design and produce their own books on subjects within the theme that most interested them. Despite the tension and sometimes resistance around teacher training, I don't regret the decision. Teachers to this day are using many of the techniques and methods that Dr. Schluck taught them. These have been passed down to new teachers and are an integral part of the thematic teaching at our school which will be discussed in detail in chapter seven.

Board Chair Mary Markin worked tirelessly for the school. She was totally committed to the success of the school. However, once I was hired as the principal, it was difficult for her to let go of the control. She didn't approve of some of my decisions. This is a typically hard transition in a charter school when the founding board chair does not become the school director and has to relinquish the reins to someone else who will inevitably do things differently. The tension was understandable but difficult for a new principal who needed guidance and support. On the positive side, this tension forced me to trust my own thinking and move forward based on it.

At every board meeting, I presented a written principal's report. I started this practice early on because too many things that I reported verbally did not end up in the minutes. This resulted in my written report being attached to the minutes which made them a better record of what was happening as we moved forward in planning the school. These reports have proven invaluable when trying to research the history of our school's progress.

Just as the new charter school movement represented a coalition of different political viewpoints, so did our founding board. One of my first conflicts with the founding board as the newly hired principal was over the issue of diversity in the school. Although my voice shook as I spoke to the board, I was adamant that in order to show that our innovative teaching methods worked, we had to have a school population that reflected the racial and economic diversity of our community. On another level, I wondered how we could teach and model respect in a multicultural world if we were an all-white school. When I looked at the list of families who had signed on, they were almost all white and middle class. I pushed for using a select lottery system to provide some racial and socioeconomic balance. The board chair and the business manager were adamant that we could not use any type of select lottery or we would be charged with discrimination. The majority on the board (which had only white members at that time) agreed that only a straight lottery would suffice.

I lost the first battle...and the second. I couldn't let the issue die though. I usually think of myself as fairly timid in my relationship with the board during those early months as a new principal, but on this issue of paramount importance, I was persistent. I did not think that we could accomplish what we wanted without a diverse school community. It was a make or break issue for me. I did not want to be the principal of an all-white school, so I went to the person who served as our charter school liaison with the Leon County School District and asked him for help. Dr. Jim Croteau assured me that it was the district's expectation that we serve a diverse population. He helped me write an enrollment policy that would stay true to the state law that required a lottery for enrollment but would aim us toward the goal of 30 percent non-white students. Basically, the first 70 percent would be drawn in a general lottery after which we would use select lotteries to insure that our school population mirrored the district averages.

I took the draft policy to the board. It was the third time that I had raised this issue, but because it had the school district's backing, they agreed to accept the policy because "it was the right thing to do." There was still some mumbling that we might be sued, but it was decided. We later amended the charter to include a commitment to reflecting the diversity of the larger Tallahassee community.

As it turned out, this was one of the most important decisions that the board made in creating the character of our school. Since the school's original organizers were all white, it was difficult at first to be trusted by communities of color. In the early years, we advertised in minority communities and spoke at community centers, but once we had established a diverse population in the school, it was self-sustaining. People talked to their friends about how well the school worked for their children and before long, there were very few select lotteries because the initial drawings maintained the diversity of our school.

After working hard all summer to get the teachers hired and trained, I took off for ten days in Montana. I was totally exhausted from tumultuous summer weeks of hiring and training teachers, working with the board, making decisions and planning for the opening of school. I arrived hours after midnight following a long plane ride across the country and a drive in a rental car up a long gravel road to the rustic log cabin that I had rented deep in the Montana wilderness. Although I owned land in Montana, there was currently no structure on the property which resulted in my renting a cabin from a friend. I could smell the sharp evergreen fragrance of the woods as I stumbled through the chilly dark night to the little cabin with no electricity or running water. As I closed the heavy handmade wooden door behind me, I dropped my bags and sank to the floor sobbing. It had been a summer that had tested me in every way possible, but now I was home in the place where my heart felt nourished and comforted. It was at that moment that I let myself totally feel the stress of the new project. Although I had been spending my summers there since 1979, this summer I only gave myself ten days to slow down and find myself again before the new school year began. Gazing at the high mountains, breathing the cool, dry air, sticking my bare feet into icy streams, and hiking with friends, I reclaimed my body and my spirit, and got ready to open a new school.

On the heels of my return, the big crisis came in late July, just a few weeks before the teachers would start work, when the owners of the downtown building backed out of the agreement. They had decided that a school would not be compatible with the other offices that they rented nearby. The local paper, the *Tallahassee Democrat*, carried several stories during the next few weeks about our attempt to find a home.

We were frantic! It was a race against time. We furiously looked for another building and found a day care facility that was available for lease. However, in order to occupy the building, the school would have to go through the city's review process to address traffic and environmental concerns. The process would take months. Mayor Scott Maddox asked city officials to speed up the process, but there was not enough time before the first day of school in August. This was a crushing disappointment for everyone. The parents who had worked so hard had their hopes dashed. The students who were registered for our school had to register at other schools. The teachers who had been hired found themselves without jobs. This included me.

Although we were all devastated, the board chair took it the hardest and as a result resigned from the board. She sent her letter of resignation to members of the charter school board and the district school board. Her resignation was reported in the local newspaper and sent us into a panic. We were afraid that the Leon County School Board would rescind their support for our school. We appealed to them to postpone our opening for one year and they agreed to do so. Dr. Roger Pinholster became the new board chair.

When I look back now from the perspective of having created an outstanding school, it seems reasonable that we continued. However, at the time, it was just short of miraculous that we pushed forward against all of the obstacles. Our dream was in tatters. I, for one, longed to run back to Montana and leave it all behind. However, we never gave up. The board members, teachers, and parents who were committed to this project were models of persistence. We never considered for one moment that we couldn't make it happen. The dream lived on despite our great disappointment.

I met with our now unemployed teachers. We were all scrambling to find other jobs for the school year. I told them that they were free to do whatever they needed to do, but that some of us were planning to stay together and open the school the following year. About half of the teachers decided to stay with the project and work toward opening the school. Everyone, including me, had to find other jobs in the meantime and this was our first priority.

I spent the next few weeks as an unemployed person for the first time in my adult life. It was terrifying. As a single mother, I worried about being able to pay my mortgage and other bills and support my daughter. There were some district teaching job openings in my field, but I didn't know if I could stand to work in a traditional school after planning for something so different. My former principal, Rosanne Wood, called Tom Dunn, the principal of Second Chance, a district program that offered students who had been expelled from school the chance to continue their education. Rosanne recommended to Tom that he hire me for an opening that he had publicized. I was offered a job as the classroom teacher at the runaway shelter at Capital City Youth Services. Tom Dunn would be my supervisor even though I would not be working on the Second Chance campus. Before accepting the job, I visited the shelter and met the young adults who ran the place. I was impressed by their optimism and positive energy and their philosophy about how young people in trouble should be treated, so I accepted the job. I wanted to work with them and my respect for them grew with every passing day.

That job was a lesson in flexibility for me because most of my students were at the shelter for only two to six days at a time. On any day, I never knew until I got there who I would have in class and how long they would stay at the shelter. I had a "one-room school" with students from twelve to sixteen years old—the ultimate multi-age classroom. We used newspapers and computers to make sure that they were reading and working on math. Although I enjoyed working with the students, I did much more counseling than teaching. Even though I wanted to spend my time working on the new charter school, this job helped to prepare me for the many unexpected things that happen when you run a school. It also provided me an income and a school day with no take-home lesson plans so that I had time to work on the charter school logistics after school and on weekends. I had two jobs that year: the one at the shelter that came with a salary and planning for a new charter school with no monetary compensation. I look with envy upon the start-up grants that are now available to pay principals for their planning year before a charter school opens. I wish I had had that luxury.

While working at the runaway shelter, my mind was constantly thinking ahead to the time when we would open our charter school. I met Vickey Bowens who worked in the office at Second Chance as the Registrar and enjoyed talking with her when I went by there to pick up my mail or speak to the principal. I recruited Vickey for our school's front office because she is a beautiful, vivacious, outgoing woman who has a smile that lights up the world. I thought that she would be perfect in our front office as the first person that people would meet when they came on campus. She started working at the school the summer before we opened and she is still there today.

In the fall, I traveled to Boston to visit a new charter school that had just opened that year in the Lynn community. The new principal had invited me to observe for a week. It was a very informative and inspiring week following the principal around and sitting in classrooms. The Lynn Community Charter School was an urban school with no green space although there was playground equipment on a paved section behind the school. The school served a very racially diverse working class population of students. The young, enthusiastic teaching staff was excited to be there. Although the curriculum was more traditional than we planned ours to be, there were many similarities between the vision of the school and the one that we had. It was a week well spent and I appreciated Principal Tom Dunn for allowing me the time from my job to have this experience.

Even with the disappointment of not opening in August 1998, I am glad that we had that planning year. It gave us time to further think, organize, prepare, and train. We still had a waiting list of students and parents who wanted to be a part of the school, so that was not an issue for us. I met with teachers every other week which demonstrated their continuing commitment. Between August and December, the board met weekly. The main task of the board was finding a building.

It is difficult to remember the agony and panic that we felt during those months at not having a building. When a principal opens a new district school, the building is provided by the district fully furnished and maintained. Since we were opening a charter school, our experience was much different. We were responsible for finding our own building and financing it. Every week we looked at buildings. Some of them were unbelievably run down, but we thought that we could do anything, including turn a dump into a school. We looked at hundreds of possibilities and nothing seemed to work. I appreciate Robert Metcalf from the Leon County Schools' Building and Maintenance Department, who met with us to look at numerous buildings and tell us what they would need to qualify as public schools. He must have thought we were crazy, or at least fanatics, to even consider some of those sites. One building that we were looking at was on a major highway and was absolutely filthy and full of trash. The fact that we even considered it is a testament to our optimism and trust in the boundless energy of our parent volunteers. Robert just shook his head when he saw the place. I appreciate the patience and guidance that he gave us during that time.

That fall Terry Kant-Rauch, one of our active parent volunteers, was elected to the board in order to bring her real estate experience to our search for a building. In December, she found our site while looking through listings of commercial property. Epiphany Lutheran Church was moving to a new ten-acre site because they had outgrown their sanctuary and they were selling their old site. The church had operated a private school on the property that contained a beautiful sanctuary and downstairs classrooms, a building with an office and four more classrooms, and an old house (parsonage) that had been converted into classrooms. Herman Frese, a neighbor of mine who served on the church's board of directors, helped us negotiate a deal to lease the property for the first year followed by purchase in the second year.

The only drawback to this property was that it was only big enough to house a kindergarten through eighth grade school. This meant that we had to give up, at least temporarily, the idea of having a school that went through high school. I was relieved. After working for seventeen years at SAIL High School, I knew the challenges of operating a high school. I knew that a kindergarten through eighth grade school was a big enough slice to bite off.

As I walked onto the property the first time, I had goose bumps imagining us there. I couldn't believe how lucky we were. After our search of hundreds of rundown, makeshift buildings with no playgrounds, this property was perfect. The buildings were large and nestled on four acres of hillside with towering live oaks and pines. The sanctuary, soon to be our auditorium, which dominated the center of the property had high ceilings, huge beams, and many windows. It could seat the entire school. There were plenty of parking spaces and two playgrounds. The lower playground had equipment for younger children and the upper playground had a paved basketball court. There were enough classrooms for a kindergarten through eighth grade school and a large office. It was beyond anything that we had hoped for. Our dream was coming true!

Chapter 2: The Beginning Years 1999-2003

The first day of school finally arrived. Everyone was smiling. In fact, the picture that the local newspaper carried looked like I had a huge mouth because my grin literally stretched across my entire face! We were actually giddy with excitement. Students arrived in buses and cars and the teachers greeted them as they entered their classrooms. The day was sunny and steaming hot, as only an August day in Florida can be, but we barely noticed the muggy weather. We finally had our school. Our dream had come true.

Dr. Jim Croteau, the charter school liaison with Leon County Schools at that time, was on campus as the students arrived. He commented that our first day started out smoothly and added that this is not always the case with new schools. We had planned well for the first day and it showed. Our teacher planning days prior to the first day of school had been three weeks long. Students had attended what we called a "Get Acquainted Social" the Friday before the first day of school so they had already met their teachers and seen their classrooms. In addition, each teacher had met individually with each of their students' families prior to the first day.

Everything was not perfect, however. Because of the church's timetable for turning over the property to us, we only gained access to the buildings a few weeks before school started. In addition, money had been short and we started the first day without tables and chairs in many of the classrooms. The only three computers in the whole school were in the office. Unlike a district school where the building is built and equipped by the district, we were on our own to figure out how to finance everything until the first official student count in October when we would start receiving public funds. These were the days before Federal Start-Up Grants for new charter schools. Our financial hero was our business manager, John Smith, who negotiated a bank loan for the school. With this money we could pay for our lease, utilities, salaries, and furniture until the public school funds started coming in.

Without a cafeteria, everyone brought their lunches to school. For the first few months of the first school year, classrooms ate their lunches outside which was comfortable, given Florida's climate. Lunch was a festive occasion like a family picnic with everyone sitting on blankets under the sprawling oak trees. Our parent organization started their first fundraising drive to raise money for picnic tables.

We pieced together our classroom furniture with rejects from elsewhere. We used everything that we could find, salvage, fix, or construct. We were able to find some furniture at the school district warehouse (discarded from district classrooms). Dr. Carolyn Schluck had been hoarding used classroom furniture for years to be used once the new school opened. Greg, the new science teacher, made tables from old doors and two-by-fours, which were quite rickety. Many classrooms used giant electrical spools for tables and parents built shelving to hold books and materials. Volunteers from the community with no children in the school, Terry Schneider and Bob Scanlon, worked in their home shops to build cubbies for the kindergarten through second grade classrooms and teacher mailboxes for the office. In addition, a law firm donated used furniture for the office. Actually, the entire time that I was principal, my office was furnished with those early donations. Saving money is something at which a small charter school has to be very good.

Our campus was a positive, happy place to be and the classrooms had exciting and interesting "hands on" activities that involved students in the learning process. Visitors commented on how many smiles they saw when they came on campus. Parents reported that their children loved coming to school and were sad when there was a holiday and they could not come. We knew that the learning environment that we had created was good.

Here is an excerpt from our parent newsletter, *Dragon Times*, from October of our first school year, where I answered the following question: "My child is having so much fun at School of Arts and Sciences, is he really learning anything?"

Your child is having fun because he is engaged in what is happening in his class. He is excited about learning. He wants to get out of bed and come to school every morning. Too many times, we as parents forget that learning is a joyous process because of our own bleak experiences in the educational system. You can relax. Your child is learning new and exciting things every day. Within the theme-based/hands-on approach, there are always opportunities for a cross-section of subjects to be taught and learned. Math, history, writing, reading, science, geography, and art are included in the overall themes or projects. Your son has the opportunity to explore and investigate and construct his own understandings about how the world works. He is developing a positive attitude toward the learning process and is confident in his ability to discover what he wants to know. He is learning how to take charge of his own learning. This is more valuable than a hundred worksheets.

I loved my job from the very beginning. I could hardly introduce myself as the principal of the School of Arts and Sciences without giggling in delight. There is nothing more exciting than being totally immersed in a project about which you are completely passionate. Every morning, I awoke looking forward to the challenges of the day. I saw an important part of my job being that of community builder. Before classes started each morning, I stood on the crosswalk to welcome students to school and wave to the parents who were dropping their children off. Years later, when I was still doing this, someone commented that the principal shouldn't have to be out directing traffic. I smiled and said, "I'm not directing traffic, I'm building community." Despite all of the school issues to be dealt with, the time that I spent every morning welcoming students was worth every second from my busy day. Welcoming the students set the tone for the students' day, made me visible to the parents, and kept me tuned in to the fact that relationships are important in a good school.

We started the first year with 175 students with plans to add one classroom of 25 students during each of the next two years. We had to use a lottery the very first year that we opened because we had more people who wanted to send their children than we had room. Our lottery pool continued to grow every year. Unfortunately, there were those who decided not to send their children the first year that we opened. They preferred to wait to see whether or not we were successful. While this caution was totally understandable, some of them missed their opportunity and were never lucky enough to be drawn in the lottery a few years later.

Parents were taking a gamble to put their children into a new school with unproven leadership and a different model of organizing and facilitating classrooms. They were courageous and involved. One parent commented happily that her children were "guinea pigs" in this new educational frontier. Others who heard her statement were horrified by this idea and worried that they were making a mistake. The teachers worked hard to alleviate these fears.

Much planning and preparation went into the first day of school. Not only did teachers meet together for a year before our school opened, but we had three weeks of pre-planning and the entire staff was paid for their time. This was absolutely necessary since we were creating this school from the dreams and ideas in our minds including all of the procedures for running the school. During those three weeks, we met as a staff every morning, leaving the rest of the day for teachers to work in their classrooms or meet as teams to develop thematic curriculum.

I began the first teacher planning session in the first year that our school opened by saying:

"The success or failure of this project rides on the quality of the relationships that we have with each other."

I knew that to develop a climate of respect at our school, we had to start with ourselves, the teachers and staff. I explained that how we treated each other would be a model for the students and their families. I asked the teachers and staff to make a commitment to each other. I asked us all to promise that whenever things got difficult with someone else on the staff that we would talk directly to that person and try to resolve it together rather than resorting to gossip or criticism.

I knew from experience that teachers in many schools tend to talk about each other behind their backs. Many of them criticize, gossip, complain, judge, and get their feelings hurt. How can there be a climate of respect in the school when this is happening among the teachers? We needed a new way of working together that relied on the commitment to talk directly and honestly to one another. Although there will always be "stuff" that comes up between people who work closely with each other, we needed to plan ahead for what we would do when it happened. I taught the teachers a format called the "Listening Exchange" where they took turns talking and listening while they worked through a difficulty. This pledge to talk directly to each other when there was a difficulty became the cornerstone of our program to create a respectful campus. During the first day of pre-planning in the first year, and every year afterwards, we made this pledge to each other.

Empowering the teachers was one of my goals with the new school. In the mornings of our first pre-planning weeks, I facilitated a process that helped us write the first procedures for how our school would run. One meeting we would brainstorm ideas regarding a particular set of procedures, such as how we would deal with a disruptive student or how attendance records would be kept and reported. Before the next morning, I would develop the wording for the procedures based on the ideas that had been generated. At that meeting, the teachers would either approve the procedures as written or, more often, suggest more changes. I would take these ideas and edit the procedures and bring them back to the group the following morning. We simultaneously worked on several different sets of procedures. The cooperative spirit was incredible. There are more details about how collaborative leadership worked at our school in chapter nine.

Eventually, all of the draft procedures were approved and we were ready on the first day of school with new procedures that everyone had participated in developing. Needless to say, we did not know enough to write procedures about everything during that first pre-planning period. For instance, although the morning of the first day of school went smoothly, we suddenly realized that we had not developed a plan for student dismissal at the end of the day. I hurriedly put a dismissal process together and circulated it among the teachers. We experimented with the new process at the end of the day and all of the gaps in the plan were quickly observed. After much feedback from teachers and various revisions to the plan, we had a smooth process for dismissal by the end of the first week.

As things happened throughout the school year, we continued to write procedures to cover these issues. Teachers met together each day for "tea time" to check in with each other and refine our school procedures. For me, one of the hardest things about our first year was the lack of a comprehensive set of policies and procedures. In seemed as though every day brought ten new things that had to be figured out and handled. I have never made so many decisions as I did that first year.

At some point, we realized the difference between policies and procedures. Many of the procedures that we had written as a staff became school policies that were approved by the board. We learned that the board makes policy and the staff makes procedures based on the policies. This understanding helped to clarify the different roles of the board and the staff. For example, day-to-day operations are the responsibility of the principal, such as setting the daily schedule, hiring staff, and evaluating teachers, while the board's roles include financial oversight, constructing new buildings, and evaluating the principal. After a number of years, we started to get these roles straightened out.

When we get ready to replicate our school in the future, we will probably start with the policies and procedures that have already been developed, but in that first year there was no blueprint for what we were doing. In addition, we were trying to create a school that belonged to all of us. Years of working with a consensus process in activist organizations gave me the patience to sustain this long process and to refrain from feelings of attachment to my drafts. The final outcome was the best thinking of the entire group. There was very little grumbling among teachers about these procedures because everyone had worked on them together in a collaborative process. In subsequent years, the process was not so difficult because we only needed to refine or revise what we already had. The reason that this process worked so well was that the entire staff was committed to working together to create our school.

*****

One unexpected development was the animosity of the adjoining neighborhood. Our students were generally well-behaved and respectful, so we could not understand why some of the neighbors were against us being there. Then we discovered that the neighborhood problem pre-dated us; we had innocently inherited it from the church. Believing in peace and people's ability to solve problems, we met with the neighborhood group before the first day of school. What we learned from our irate neighbors was that the church school's car traffic had lined up through the neighborhood blocking their driveways every morning when students were being dropped off at school. To show that we wanted to be good neighbors, we routed our traffic a different way so that our parents' cars would not back-up through the neighborhood. This, however, did not appease the neighborhood activists because our traffic left the school and traveled through the neighborhood. We researched other ways to handle our traffic, but the city and state authorities working with us did not see any other solution because of the small size of our campus. Believing that relationships are important, we met with the neighborhood association to try to resolve the issues, but the neighborhood issue plagued us for many years.

The neighbor whose property adjoined our upper playground was continually coming onto school property to yell at the students on the basketball court. Granted, the students were making noise as they played outside during recess, but it was the normal joyful sounds of children playing. We counseled our students to not respond to her curses and threats. Some of the students baked cookies for her during the after school program and took them to her, but this didn't solve the problem. We eventually built a tall wooden privacy fence to separate our campus and protect our students from this neighbor. When she came around the fence to confront students, we decided to get a trespassing warrant in order to ensure the safety of our students. In later years, she began a campaign of saving urine to throw over the fence. It smelled awful and we had to talk to a police officer about the issue. He spoke to her on our behalf. She escalated by letting a sewage pipe run toward the fence. As a result, we had to call the City Health Department about the violation.

While this neighbor's tactics were by far the worst that we encountered, others in the neighborhood found different ways to protest our existence. A complaint by a neighbor resulted in our receiving a citation for violating the city landscape ordinance that required that we have shrubs or fences to shield our campus from the neighborhood. Having recently acquired the property, we were not aware of any landscape violations but we moved quickly to meet the requirement that cost us many thousands of dollars that we had not anticipated.

I had been working for more than a year without compensation (before the school opened) when the board negotiated an eleven-month contract with me with a salary that was higher than what had been advertised in the newspaper to attract applicants. I was thrilled with the contract because it gave me a month during the summer to be in Montana. I loved the long dusty gravel road leading from a small town to this isolated area teeming with wildlife tucked up close to the Canadian Border. I am one of those people who need wilderness to stay whole. I could work twelve-hour days during the entire school year without a single complaint as long as I could count on some uninterrupted time in the wilderness. I need to be able to gaze at a landscape unobstructed by pavement and buildings and electric lights. Time off to be in Montana was more important to me than salary, so the 11-month contract suited me.

My contract was for two years, after which time the contract could be renegotiated if the board wanted to retain me. There was to be a $2000 bonus for me at the end of two years if the school met the academic goals set out in the charter application. Board Chair Roger Pinholster reiterated that the board's expectation was that I commit to staying on the job for at least two years. I think that he was worried about the possibility that I might quit after the first year because of the work load. When he said that, I looked at him in surprise because my intention was to stick with the project until I retired from education and that was at least a decade away. One thing that I knew about myself was that I was not a quitter. This was a good thing because little did I know how rocky the road ahead would be.

In December of our first year, we held a ceremony in the auditorium. The entire school was there along with invited guests who included the district superintendent and the district school board. Students had made paper hands that stretched around the entire auditorium. There was a ribbon cutting by Board Chair Roger Pinholster. We held a reception for the guests following the ceremony. A few years later, the auditorium was dedicated to two of the school's founders, Drs. Carolyn and Gerry Schluck, whose vision was instrumental in the school becoming a reality. There is a sign honoring them on the front of the auditorium.

We learned a lot that first year. We were all very excited about implementing a hands-on, thematic curriculum, but we naively forgot how much time and work it takes for teachers to develop their own curriculum. Insecurities plagued us during this early period. We felt like we were not sure what we were doing. Mary DeHoff, one of our early teachers, said that if she could go back in time, the one thing that she would change would be to insist that we stop saying that we didn't know what we were doing. In looking back, it is easy to see the vigor with which we moved forward. However, at the time we were exploring new territory, trying new things, and stepping out of our comfort zones that left us feeling like we didn't know what we were doing. These were just feelings and this is a good example of how feelings are not reality; they are just feelings. In addition to feeling inept, we had set up a schedule that did not give teachers any real planning time during the school day.

They were with their students all day long including lunch and recess. We were quickly on our way to burning out the teaching staff.

Things were not much better for the administrative staff because we had only three people (business manager, office manager, and principal) to do everything during the first two years. Actually, the founders had envisioned no office manager or receptionist in the front office, only a principal teacher (who would be teaching much of the day) and a business manager. They thought that the teachers could answer their own phone calls, keep their own attendance records, manage visitors, etc. This is where experience in a small private school does not translate into what is required in a larger public school. There has to be office staff to protect the classrooms from constant interruption and to handle the tremendous amount of paperwork that is required in a public school. One case in point is the verification and tracking of student enrollment and attendance. The allocation of public funds is based on student enrollment and the state doesn't just take your word for how many students you have. Our district had a computerized way of tracking this and we were required to send our office manager, Vickey Bowens, to training and use their system to verify our enrollment and attendance. Besides that, there were personnel and student records to maintain, as well as purchase orders and other accounting details that had to be tracked meticulously. The school facilities and grounds had to be maintained and cleaned. Schedules had to be developed.

Logistics regarding buses and lunches had to be managed. A clinic had to be available for children who were ill. The list of administrative responsibilities seemed endless.

I had hoped that we could keep the office staff down to a minimum in order to put as many resources as possible into the classrooms. We had a business manager who handled the finances and the school operations (repairs, maintenance, etc.). We had an office manager who managed the office, the clinic, and the records (including schedules, attendance, and personnel). I did the jobs of the principal, assistant principal, guidance counselor, curriculum coordinator, and test coordinator. And we relied on hundreds of volunteer hours from parents and board members. Two parents and board members, Terry Kant-Rauch and Lyn Kittle, handled the entire admissions process because there was no time for the limited office staff to get the work done. They and others also helped to develop forms and e-mail lists, and worked on communications and the website. We would not have made it without all of the volunteer help. It was not humanly possible to handle the mountain of work.

It is sometimes difficult to remember how hard we had to work during those first few years. The days were filled with so many things that sometimes I was shocked that it was time for student dismissal when it seemed like the day had just begun. I worked seven days a week and was often still at school at ten pm on weeknights when my daughter was with her father. At that time, we had couches in the conference room and I joked about just staying all night and sleeping on the couch. Although I never did that, it was almost impossible to be absent (for illness or anything else) those first few years because new decisions had to be made every day and I was the only one in the office who had educational leadership experience. When I was sick, I still had to come to work. When I came to work ill, I would work behind a closed door to keep from exposing others as much as possible, but I was available for making decisions and handling emergencies. The school came first. There were many things in my life, such as dating and gardening, which I gave up in order to do this job well in those first hectic years. I was a beginning principal in a brand new school and the learning curve was steep.

During those early years, I sometimes found it difficult to take good care of myself. Before becoming a principal, I had led many workshops on the topic of alleviating burnout for educators, but I had to force myself to take my own advice during the early years of the school. I knew a leader needed to be well rested, well nourished, and well exercised in order to be as effective as possible. While I did my best at the school, I continually functioned on top of a lack of sleep and exercise. Although I was committed to eating healthy food, I often forgot to eat lunch during the busy days at school. Then, I would eat the food that I had brought for lunch in the evening and keep on working into the night. I lost weight from the wrong reasons—stress, overwork, and forgetting to eat. In addition, although I usually relied on co-counseling sessions (trading counseling time with a partner) to release emotion in order to keep my brain functioning clearly, I was even skimping on that because there was so much work to be done. My constant solace was my weeks of summer vacation time in Montana that soothed and relaxed me. I placed a huge picture of Glacier National Park on a wall in my office that reminded me to take deep breaths and relax during the frenetic school year.

I was not alone in making these sacrifices. Many people made many sacrifices during the beginning years of our school. One person who never gets any credit for making sacrifices for the school was my daughter. Emma was just finishing middle school and starting high school during our school's beginning years. I must admit that she missed out on a lot of quality time with her mom during those years when I was staying at school late and working on weekends. She handled the situation with a positive attitude and her dad, who had shared custody, took up some of the slack, but having her mom so preoccupied with the school was hard for her. Given the circumstances, I don't know what I could have done differently, but I can admit that it was not the best situation for her. Not being available for her as much as I could is my biggest regret about taking on this project. Parental guilt, the constant companion of parents, was with me during this time.

I was not the only one who was overworking. The teachers were suffering under the load of creating thematic curriculum and having no planning period. Pure passion and adrenalin kept us going, but we were sure to crash eventually.

Working with two board members, Roger Pinholster and Rosanne Wood, who were also principals with the district, I developed a special area schedule that would accomplish two things—add the arts into the curriculum and give the teachers a planning period once a day. This was met with great relief by the teachers. One of our teachers, Julie Fredrickson, deserves special note because she was not only a lead teacher, but also the music teacher during the first year. In addition, we hired part-time art teacher Mandy Rozier and drama teacher Eden Rush as special area teachers to create planning time for classroom teachers.

We also had a huge parent volunteer program which provided a considerable amount of relief for teachers. Parents supervised students on the playgrounds in the mornings before school so that teachers could get their classrooms ready for learning. In addition, many parents supervised students during lunch to give teachers more time for planning and organizing materials. In the spring, a parent donated a beach house on St. George Island near Tallahassee and the parent organization provided food for a weekend teacher retreat. The big, gorgeous beach house was surrounded by snowy-white sand and faced the blue-green waters of the Gulf of Mexico. This soothing environment provided the teachers and me a weekend away from campus to relax and work together on thematic curriculum and team building. Not all of the teachers stayed for the entire weekend due to family responsibilities, but they were all there for Saturday. Julie Fredrickson brought

Orff instruments from the music program and we played music in the evening and performed for the students the following week. As hard as the first year was, the teachers received a tremendous amount of support and appreciation from parents.

*****

While board members were generally pleased with the progress that the school was making, there were some tensions between some of the founders and some of the newer board members who held different perspectives on where the school was heading. One founder was particularly critical in his descriptions of how the school in reality was different from what he had envisioned. His remarks were often insulting and inflammatory and directed toward me, but I chose to listen carefully and calmly and not get into arguments with him. On the other hand, two newer board members made a decision to interrupt every negative comment with a positive perspective. Their decision to do so kept the board on an even keel during these early years.

There were many surprises during our first year. One thing that surprised me was that the students wanted to have a school mascot. I had always thought that mascots were primarily for sports teams and we didn't have any of those. However, the students were excited about having an election to choose a mascot. Many ideas were brainstormed and many of the adult members of our school community were afraid that our mascot was going to be "Monkeys" because some of the middle school students were pushing hard for that. However, the imaginations of younger students won out and "Dragons" received the most votes. We have used the Dragon logo on school t-shirts and newsletters. A chainsaw artist carved a wooden dragon sculpture using an oak tree stump at the entrance of the school. In this beautiful piece of sculpture, the friendly-looking dragon is sitting on a stack of books holding a paint brush and a magnifying glass to represent arts and sciences.

During our first year, when we were leasing the property from the church, they were still using the sanctuary on Sundays while they were constructing their new sanctuary on their new property. As a result, we were not allowed to change or renovate the building and it had a huge cross and altar in the front. Because we were a public school, we did not refer to these religious symbols in our programs, but they remained while we were leasing the building during our first year. The sanctuary retained its aura of mystery and reverence due to the subdued lighting, the dark walls, and tinted windows. It also was filled with church pews. We used the sanctuary on Fridays for our weekly school-wide assembly program called Friday Sing. When the students entered the building for Friday Sing, all of the chattering stopped and there was a reverent quietness; the only voices were hushed whisperings. Many young people are conditioned to be quiet in church and I often wonder if we shouldn't have left the building like that after we purchased it.

At the end of our first year, we were poised to purchase our property. Our charter approval would expire after the following year and the bank wanted proof of more longevity in order to give us the loan to purchase. We went back to the Leon County School Board to ask for an extension. Because our first year had been so successful, they granted us a five-year extension to the original two years remaining on the charter. We could now tell the bank that we had approval to operate for seven years. This helped us secure the loan. The property now belonged to the School of Arts and Sciences Foundation.

After the property belonged to us, we began in earnest to renovate. We worked on better accessibility to every building. We improved classroom spaces. Best of all, the sanctuary was transformed into an auditorium with a stage. The church took their cross and alter with them. Although the church pews stayed, more light was let in through clear glass windows and clear glass hanging lamps. The walls were lightened and the auditorium had less of a reverent feel to it. To this day, our auditorium is the place where we celebrate our school community every week and honor the individual talents that each one brings.

*****

In the beginning of our second year, we were not only the new owners of our school property, but we were taking ownership in our future as well. On the October Teacher Planning Day, the teachers and I had a retreat at Wakulla

Springs, sponsored by the school's parent organization, which focused on thematic instruction and team building. A week later, the school community met to use a process called PATH (Planning Alternative Tomorrows with Hope) facilitated by Dr. Roger Pinholster, a founder, board member, and district principal. A group of thirty parents, teachers, students, and board members met one evening to develop a five-year plan for the school. Roger encouraged us to dream big and we created a colorful mural that represented our goals for the future. The result was six goals: increase volunteerism, acquire vans or buses for field trips, lower class size, encourage every student to "major" in a visual or performing art, improve the playground, and increase the number of classrooms. This was an exciting community building activity that helped us organize and articulate our common dreams for the school. Although it took us longer than five years to reach some of these goals, most of them were eventually realized.

Having teacher retreats and a daily planning period did not cure everything for the teachers. They were struggling with preparing thematic lessons for their three-grade multi-age classrooms. Most of them had come from traditional schools with textbooks and prepared curriculums and it was both a challenge and a delight to create their own curriculum. What stressed them the most was the three-grade span in their classrooms. The three primary classrooms had kindergarten, first, and second graders. The three upper elementary classrooms had third, fourth, and fifth graders. The middle school classrooms had sixth, seventh, and eighth graders. Even though they had their students for three years, the teachers worried about covering all of the state standards for all those grades. Preparing lessons and activities that met the needs of such a wide age range was very hard on them.

Toward the end of the second year of the school, the teachers asked the board to consider changing from a three-grade to a two-grade multi-age configuration in the elementary classrooms. Their proposal was that during the following school year, the classes would be organized as: kindergarten and first grade together, second and third grades together, fourth and fifth grades together, and middle school classes would remain three-grades (sixth, seventh, and eighth grades). Although the board was very concerned about teacher burnout, they thought that it was too early in the development of the school to make such a major change from the original charter design. They asked that the teachers keep trying to make three grades in each classroom work and the teachers agreed because of their commitment to the school. The board promised additional training in multi-age teaching.

Knowing that the teachers needed more curriculum support and multi-age training, I hired Jane Wofford as the administrative coordinator. She would be the curriculum coordinator and oversee the school's operations, so that John, our business manager, could focus on finances. Jane had both administrative and teaching experience and we were hopeful that her efforts in the area of multi-age curriculum would help the teachers. She was a trained Montessori instructor and she began to train teachers in ways to use Montessori materials to teach basic skills in a hands-on way. We requested that the board allocate $5,000 from our reserve fund to purchase math manipulatives for the elementary classrooms. After one year of service, her job title was changed to assistant principal. I was delighted to have the expertise and experience of someone like Jane as my assistant. Jane worked with Dr. Schluck as she developed multi-age training for the teachers, but while Dr. Schluck approved of the math manipulatives, she was less than enthusiastic about the use of other Montessori materials.

This set the stage for a build-up of tension between the two. Dr. Schluck believed that she should be solely in charge of teacher training and there were others on the board that agreed with this. There was a fear among some that we were moving away from the founders' vision for thematic, multi-age instruction. At times, I felt caught between opposing forces without understanding quite what the problem was. In my mind, we were working as hard as possible to implement thematic, multi-age instruction. These tensions were the whisperings of a power struggle that would become more evident in future years during the transition stage of the school. Additional support for multi-age training was offered through a grant from the Rintels Foundation to hire Susan Smith, the founder of the Magnolia School, for one year to help teachers plan multi-age curriculum. Everyone was happy with the chance to have Susan's expertise and help because she was recognized by all as someone who had put theory into practice in her own private school. I was relieved to have Susan on staff because the teachers often expressed dissatisfaction with both Dr. Schluck's and Jane's style and I wanted to find the right kind of support for them.

*****

Better communication throughout the school community was an issue that we worked diligently to improve. Technology helped us do this. Although we had scarce resources, we were moving forward in the area of technology during our beginning years. We started our school with only three computers, but gradually increased the numbers mostly through donations and grants. Being included on the district's server and having district e-mail addresses increased our ability to communicate with each other and share documents. Before the school opened, Lyn Kittle started a parent e-mail list and sent updates to parents weekly. This was cutting-edge thinking on her part as computer communication with large groups of people was in its early stages of development in the society at large. She also worked to develop a school website to facilitate communication inside and outside our school community. "Morning Announcements" were composed by me and sent to all staff members by e-mail. I noticed that fewer things fell through the cracks when teachers requested things in writing by sending an e-mail. In June 2001, all of the classrooms were finally wired for the Internet which greatly improved the students' ability to research for their projects and presentations. By the spring of 2003, the entire school was connected through Internet.

The ability to communicate through e-mail was a significant advancement for our school. In the first year or two, the biggest complaint about my leadership was "lack of follow through." As I moved around campus, teachers and parents were always talking to me about different issues that they wanted me to do something about. Keeping all of these things in my mind was a constant struggle. Even when I tried keeping a notebook, staying on top of all of the issues was difficult. My lack of follow-through was not the result of not working hard enough. Rather, the problem was that I was overwhelmed by the amount of work required to manage the school and the lack of easy communication. A combination of reaching for a higher level of organization coupled with e-mail communication changed that significantly. When people could e-mail their requests and suggestions to me, few things fell through the cracks. My motto became: If it's not in writing, it doesn't exist.

Most parents enroll their children in a school and just accept the school's way of doing things. Things were different at our new school. Even before our school opened, parents felt that they were an integral part of charting the school's course. There were both advantages and disadvantages to this. In the early days, there were so many things being figured out that parents felt empowered to have a voice on one hand, but many felt very insecure that more things were not already in place and frustrated when things developed differently than what they wanted. Although empowering parents was one of our goals, it was not possible to include parents in every decision that was made. There was a buildup of tension around how decisions should be made and confusion regarding the parents' role in this process.

In early 2001, board member Jayme Harpring worked with a committee of community members to develop a decision-making process for the school. The flow chart that was developed clearly outlined the channels for any person in the school community to propose changes to policy or address concerns, as well as who had final decision-making power. This process was adopted by the board and was incorporated into school policy along with an organizational chart. The decision-making process institutionalized our belief that everyone should have a voice in the running of the school. At the same time, the document clarified that final decision-making authority rested with the principal and, ultimately, with the board. Giving everyone a clear way to affect changes in the school helped to alleviate some of the parent grumbling that was occurring. Because parents had had the opportunity from the very beginning to participate in setting up the school, many felt entitled to critique and offer suggestions at every turn. The decision-making chart outlined the way to do this in a constructive manner.

*****

We struggled in many ways those first few years, but the biggest challenges came during our third year. The school year of 2001-2002 was a challenging time for us and is known as "the year of floods and fire." Luckily, there was no famine or pestilence (unless you count the occasional outbreaks of lice that typically occur in elementary schools).

During the 2001-2002 school year, Tallahassee had three ten-inch rainstorms (two caused by tropical storms and one a heavy spring storm) which created flooding on our sloped school property at three different times. The water entered several classrooms and ruined books, carpets, and materials. Not only was this a major expense since flood insurance was not included in our policy, but the solution to the problem required much engineering and dirt moving to design a method for dealing with the massive water that ran through our property during torrential rains. We did not even know that our property was vulnerable in this way because previous years had not seen these big storms.

It should be noted that charter schools are on their own when disasters happen. Although they are part of the public school system, they stand alone in the area of finances, insurance, maintenance, and repair. Charter schools have to be self-reliant and cannot count on the school district or Department of Education to come to the rescue when something unexpected happens.

The first tropical storm hit during summer vacation in June and flooded three classrooms. All of the carpets were ruined and had to be replaced. One of the teachers, Julie Fredrickson, lost many books in her flooded classroom; many of them were from her private collection for student use. We did not have the funds to replace her books. After the first storm, teachers were careful to keep books and materials off the bottom of shelves or confined to plastic bins.

The second disaster resulted from Tropical Storm Barry that hit in early August, the weekend before the teacher planning week. Teachers returned to school with a flood of muddy water across the lower part of campus that blocked the entrance driveway completely. We entered campus through the exit from the adjoining neighborhood. Rainwater was literally pouring into the same classrooms that had been flooded in June. Jon Copps (a parent), Bob Beck (a teacher's husband), and Lee Ann Beam (an associate teacher) dug trenches in the mud to channel the water pouring off the back off the property and cascading down the slope. Teachers Mary DeHoff, Julie Fredrickson, and Kristn Yates went after sandbags and most of the other teachers used the shop vac, mops, and towels to sop up the water that was coming into the building. The carpets were saved and I referred to this challenge in my principal's report to the board as a "team building activity." Despite the positive spin, this was the harbinger of more disasters.

No sooner had school started than several of the neighborhood ladies started blocking our buses as they tried to leave campus after dropping off students in the morning. They were protesting the fact that our buses traveled through their neighborhood twice a day. Neighbors had put their cars in the road and would not allow the buses to pass. Several of our buses and cars had to turn around and exit out our entrance on a busy highway. This created a very dangerous traffic situation. We called the police and tried to reason with the neighbors. We were finally able to convince them to move their cars to let the buses out after the police showed up.

That afternoon, the road was once more blocked by the cars of several mothers and children holding picket signs. They backed our buses and cars up and let them through one by one so that they could tell them what their protest was about. The news media covered the story and interviewed both the protesters and me. A police officer arrived and informed them that the road is a public road and therefore it was illegal to block it or stop cars to talk to drivers. Several of our parents lived in the neighborhood, including Jane Dobbs (the president of our parent organization and also a member of the neighborhood board). They were upset about the protest and said that they had not been informed that this was going to happen. These parents told us that most of the neighborhood was supportive of the school.

As a result of this protest, our parents formed a Neighborhood Outreach Team to go door-to-door with a "Listening Project" to make contact with neighbors and listen to their concerns. The focus of their outreach efforts were on the eleven households in the neighborhood that were the most affected by our traffic. A mailing to the entire neighborhood offered to send a parent on the Neighborhood Outreach Team to discuss any concerns that they might have about our school. This resulted in only one call to the school. The call was from a neighbor who said that he had lived in the neighborhood for 35 years, that he supported our school, that there were only a few people trying to stir up trouble, and that if there was anything that he could do for us that we should ask.

The day after the neighborhood protest was September 11, 2001, and the events that occurred left all Americans stunned and grieving. Many of the parents of our students worked for state government and there was some worry that day that state capitols around the country might be attacked also. I spoke to every classroom in an effort to keep everyone calm and answered questions that the students had. Some of the youngest ones were confused by the neighborhood protest against us the day before followed by an attack on our country. In their young minds, they somehow equated the two. Others were worried about their parents working in state office buildings. Others wanted to just be reassured that we would be all right. Despite my own feelings on that day, I confidently told class after class that we were going to be OK. While it took some effort to be relaxed and confident in the face of the video showing planes slamming into the Twin Towers, I knew that reassurance was what the students needed from me that day.

That afternoon when some students were playing basketball on the upper playground, our adjoining neighbor ran out and yelled at the students saying that they were "little heathens and they should be on their knees praying" on a day like this. The students were shaken by the encounter. It was as though a miasma of fear had descended upon the school. We seemed to be under assault from all sides—neighbors, terrorists, even nature.

The school's worst disaster was yet to come. On Halloween Night, an electrical malfunction started a fire in one of the classrooms. Luckily, there was no heating or air conditioning on in the building and the fire quickly ran out of oxygen. However, the fire smoldered all night flooding the adjacent classrooms and the office with smoke through the air ducts. I was in the shower when the coordinator of the before-school program called my home to give me the news. I missed the call and did not realize that we had had a fire until I arrived on campus that morning and saw the fire trucks with their flashing lights. I was told about the fire and was hit with a numbing sense of shock. However, as the school leader, I immediately went into "take charge mode" and brushed away the feelings of anguish and disbelief that threatened to overwhelm me. The scene inside the burned classroom was grisly. The contents of the classroom were a black, melted mess, but the fire had not spread or damaged the structure of the building. Inside the classroom, computers, clocks, and anything plastic were melted into misshapen forms like a Salvador Dali painting. Papers, books, and folders were burned and/or dripping with fire retardant. Since the electricity was no longer functional, work spotlights had been set up and the harsh glow on the burned and melted objects in the room made the classroom seem like a ghoulish crime scene.

We quickly had to deal with where to put the classes before the students arrived for the school day. In addition to the main office, three other elementary classrooms besides the burned one had been "smoked." Inspectors told us that besides the burned classroom, which had to be completely gutted and rebuilt, the entire duct system in the building must be replaced. In the meantime, we could not use the heater and the windows had to be opened to air out the spaces. The fire displaced four classrooms, a total of 100 students, which was almost half of the student body. These classes met in the auditorium while we figured out what to do for the next two months while the renovations took place.

Help was on the way though. The Leon County School District loaned us a portable classroom and the City of Tallahassee agreed to give us a temporary permit to set it up in our parking lot. This provided space for the students from the burned out classroom. The Piedmont Park Alliance Church next door allowed one of our classrooms to meet in their facility. One classroom moved into the tiny art room and art moved from class to class on a cart. The other elementary classroom moved into the middle school math classroom, while middle school math was held outside on the back patio. Luckily, the weather in Tallahassee in November is just about perfect and the warm days went into December as well. I don't think that it rained a single time during the school day during our relocation. On cool mornings, the math teacher had hot chocolate waiting for the students in their outdoor patio classroom. While the classrooms in the other buildings were unaffected by the smoke, we continued to work in the smoky-smelling office with the windows open. We had no other choice.

This was a hard time for our school community and everyone struggled to find the joy that was always so evident on our campus. The teachers in the affected classrooms lost their lessons and materials and had to scramble to create new ones. They persevered in small, cramped spaces to continue to teach their students. They exhibited courage and stamina through the discouragement and inconvenience. They stayed positive and hopeful for their students and the school. They held things together when things could have fallen disastrously apart. Getting through these difficulties was heroic and everyone played a significant role by keeping the tone positive and doing what had to be done to get through this. Setting up "listening exchanges" at the beginnings of staff meetings was one way that we gave teachers the chance to vent their frustrations so that they could keep a positive perspective despite the adversity.

Likewise, these were hard times for me as a relatively new school leader. It seemed that as soon as we recovered from one disaster, another one came along and hit us in the face. I felt like it was my job to hold everything together, as well as to hold out hope in the face of everyone's discouragement. During our third year, my positive attitude was tested almost to its limits. Luckily, I had regular co-counseling sessions (the exchange of listening time with another person outside of school) where I could fall apart in private while holding out a smile and a positive attitude in public. Many people throughout my life have teased me about wearing "rose-colored glasses" and they are not completely wrong in that assessment. However, during that year of disasters, my "rose-colored glasses" served me well. They represented a decision that I had made at a very early age to focus on the positive no matter what happens.

The clean-up of the smoke-damaged rooms proceeded at a slower pace than we ever imagined. The smoke smell persisted despite the replacement of heating and air conditioning ducts, replacement of ceiling tiles, several carpet cleanings, hand cleaning of every item in the rooms several times and the operation of an ozone machine. One room was also repainted. However, before the winter holidays in mid-December, classes (except the burned out classroom) moved back into their rooms. The renovations on the burned classroom were finished in January. Things settled back to normal.

We were excited to have recovered from the fire. Rather than having our dreams go up in smoke, we were like a phoenix rising from the ashes ready to move forward. The only reminders of that trying time were the asphalt patches in the parking lot where the portable was tied down and the lingering smell of smoke in some places. I would often return to my office after it was closed for the weekend and smell smoke for a few minutes. I called this "the ghost of fires past."

Our troubles weren't over, however. Things had just settled down to normal when the third huge storm hit Tallahassee in March dropping nearly ten inches of rain in a short amount of time. This happened the night before the entire school would be taking the state assessment tests. Three classrooms (that had recently returned to their rooms after the fire) were now being evacuated again due to the flood on the first morning of testing. Jane Dobbs, the president of our parent organization who lived next door to the school, called us early in the morning to report the flooding. By noon, a cleaning service had vacuumed out about 350 gallons of water from the three flooded classrooms. We were hopeful that this would save the carpets. Most of the classroom materials were in plastic containers and off the floor this time, so they were not damaged. Tables for the Monday morning FCAT testing were moved to the auditorium and to the portable, which fortunately had not yet been moved. The electricity was still hooked up to the portable so that we would have lighting and heat for Monday morning. We were becoming disaster experts! Three floods and a fire in a year left us feeling like disaster experts.

Three days after the flood, the carpets seem to be almost dry. Luckily, the weather had been cold and dry. The carpets were cleaned and deodorized by the end of the week and classes functioned normally by the following Monday. I worried that the emotional impact of the disastrous year would affect the students' test scores, but when the scores were announced, our students had performed well and we were designated an "A" school by the state of Florida. This is an example of the resilience and positive attitudes of both the teachers and the students.

The beginning years of our charter school were fraught with all kinds of challenges, but the dedication and enthusiasm of everyone involved helped us find passage through the treacherous waters on to the transition years.

Chapter 3: The Transition Years 2003-2007

Organizations and relationships start off with a honeymoon phase. This is the most exhilarating time and is characterized by happiness and hopefulness. Everything seems right, like it was meant to be. People see the best in each other and they work hard together to overcome challenges. In young organizations, as in new relationships, there comes a time of disenchantment. People start to see each other's faults and point them out. The happiness and bliss of the honeymoon phase are often overcome by disappointment because everything is not perfect and people who seemed to be perfect are found lacking. Power struggles characterize this period. Disagreement or differences of opinion that were overlooked in the honeymoon stage are glaringly obvious in this stage. This is a dangerous time for an organization, or any relationship. Work is necessary to get through this stage and many people get lost along the way. New charter schools are no exception to this pattern. Our transition period was marked by national recognition as an outstanding charter school on the one hand and internal upheaval and strife on the other.

The school's transition years began in 2003. That summer was a particularly hot and dry one in Montana, where

I had spent my summer vacation working more than relaxing. I had been living in my ten-by-ten foot cabin for three summers and had saved enough money to continue the work on a larger cabin. That summer, the walls were framed in, the roof put on, and windows and doors installed. Once the plywood sheeting was on, the cabin was completely "dried in." The foundation and floor (covered with plastic to protect it from moisture) had been waiting for my funds to accumulate. No sooner had this construction stage been completed when a devastating wildfire swept through the area a few miles north of my cabin. It was my first experience living in a community that was fighting fire. I attended meetings, helped people evacuate who were in the fire's path, and lived in the fear and smoke that permeated the valley before returning to Tallahassee toward the end of summer vacation to start the school year. Maybe spending time in a community that was dealing with a major forest fire prepared me for the upheavals that would soon engulf me at school.

When I returned to school, there was a lot that had to be accomplished before school started. Summer renovation projects were still underway and teacher planning week was only a week away. Staff personalities had started to grate on each other. My assistant principal, Jane Wofford, was not happy because she had worked all summer while I was away. I tried to smooth things over the best I could.

My relationship with Jane was a complicated one. She exuded confidence and spoke with conviction. I appreciated her expertise and self-assurance. I believe that a good leader should surround oneself with highly qualified people and not feel threatened by their abilities. I worked hard to avoid indulging in my own insecurities because I understood that this was a manifestation of internalized sexism that undermines the relationship between many women leaders. However, many staff members and parents felt diminished by her attitude toward them and they were not hesitant to tell me about this. I found myself in the position of defending her time and time again.

The campus was not ready for the start of school when I returned from Montana; we were in the middle of many big renovations, including a new ramp to improve accessibility. As often happens in construction, things were running behind schedule. The middle school had received many improvements such as new floors and paint and best of all, new lockers that the students had been clamoring for. In all fairness, I think Jane's dissatisfaction stemmed from having worked all summer while I was in Montana. The fact was that I had an eleven month contract that required me to be gone for one month. My vacation time had to be taken in the summer because I needed to be on campus when school was in session. Jane's job included management of the buildings and grounds and that work had to take place during the summer break when classes were not in session. This arrangement set us up for some resentment that sometimes bubbled up in the presence of others and would ultimately be reported back to me. When viewed from her perspective, it's understandable why this might happen.

In August of 2003, at the beginning of our fifth year of operation, our business manager, John Smith, was getting ready to retire. We were sad to see him go. John had offered not only his financial expertise, but a sense of humor and attitude of good will that kept everything operating smoothly. It was decided that his financial duties would be taken over by the assistant principal and he spent time over the summer training her. This meant that she would be responsible for the finances and operations of the school and would have less time for curriculum coordination. This worked well because tension had built between Jane and the teachers and her new responsibilities removed her from working with them as directly as she had before. She brought in a whole new way of managing our finances that resulted in more efficiency. Jane was a talented woman and a hard worker and I wanted to find the right place for her and keep her on our staff.

Managing people and working with the various personalities in an organization is the hardest work that a leader does. I once commented to a board member that the only thing that was really hard about my job was dealing with people's upsets. There is a lot of work in running a school, but work is just work and can be accomplished with enough time and attention. Dealing with upset people is much harder.

I believe that people are inherently good, cooperative, loving, intelligent, and connected to everyone else. Upsets are usually triggered by old hurts from the past. Without this baggage of hurt, we would be able to see any difficult situation as an interesting challenge that could bc addressed and handled by our intelligent minds working together cooperatively. Unfortunately, we all carry deep hurts that get triggered from time to time. When we were originally hurt, our minds recorded all of the sights, sounds, smells, and feelings from the hurtful situation. When our old hurts get triggered, we act on the basis of these old, recorded feelings from the past rather than our intelligence and clear thinking in the present. What we say or do during these situations is often irrational and unhelpful. When people around us start operating on their old recorded feelings of distress, it is often difficult to continue working together in a cooperative way. I find that when faced with upset people, it's helpful to recognize the difference between a person and that person's emotional distress. That's easier said than done though.

The most challenging situations for a leader occur when a group of people organizes around someone's distress. Rather than working in a constructive, collaborative way to make changes, they organize others to join in their attack and try to undermine the direction in which things are moving. Every school has a small group of malcontents who continually take pot shots at the school's leadership. Our school was no exception. The difference is that in a large school, a small group of complainers is hardly noticed. In a small school, a small group of unhappy people can make much more noise.

During the four years of our transition period as a school, one small group created havoc whenever they found an opening. This started early in our fifth year of operation.

Upon my return from Montana that summer, I dove into twelve-hour work days seven days a week to get the campus ready for the teachers and students to return. There was a flurry of activity leading up to the board meeting that occurred during the pre-planning week. I sensed tension in the air prior to the board meeting. My thought was that there might be criticism aimed at the assistant principal, and I was prepared to defend her. However, I had no idea what was coming.

I had good news to report to the board in my principal's report. I informed the board that we had once again received an "A" grade based on our students' standardized test scores. In addition, we had met the federal standards for "No Child Left Behind," a feat which only 22 percent of the district schools had accomplished. We were definitely achieving great things.

The board meeting proceeded as usual until the last item on the agenda, "Persons to Be Heard." This is the point in the meeting when anyone can address the board on any issue that concerns him or her. A man whose children attended the school and who was married to one of the board members asked to speak. I'll call him "Mr. V" in order to tell this story and protect his anonymity. Mr. V began presenting a prepared statement that questioned my ability to be the principal. He had a long list of complaints which included my work ethic, salary, time in Montana, hiring practices, chaos from building projects, and the dissatisfaction of some middle school students. To me, his statement was full of half-truths and misjudgments and I was appalled by the way he stated them as fact. Although we subsequently instituted a three-minute limit for those wishing to speak to the board, at that time there was no such rule and the board chair allowed Mr. V to go on with his statement for fifteen minutes.

I was caught completely by surprise. There had been no prior indication that this was going to happen. No one had talked to me about any of these issues prior to the board meeting and there were not even any rumors that it would happen. I made a decision to listen intently to every word so that I would be able to address all of his issues. Although I held onto my calm demeanor, I was quite shaken. The attack was perfectly timed. We had just added many new members to the board and they did not know me yet. Mr. V was such an excellent speaker that I could tell that the new board members were persuaded by the things that he said. The lesson that I learned that night was: Always make sure that your relationship with board members is such that they know who you are and what you stand for so that they can make informed judgments about complaints against you. How to do this is discussed in chapter nine.

When his speech was over, Dr. Jim Croteau, our Leon County Schools Liaison, requested that Mr. V put his comments in writing so that I could respond to them in writing.

I was relieved by that suggestion because first of all, I was upset at that moment and secondly, he had touched on so many issues that to respond immediately would have appeared that I was being defensive. My answer to Mr. V that evening was that I did not agree with anything in his statement and that I would respond to each point in writing to the board. I added that at our school we had an agreement to talk directly to each other when there was a problem, but that there had been no attempt by Mr. V to talk to me about these issues prior to this meeting.

It is common for people in leadership roles to be attacked and often these attacks are personal in nature. Observers tend to focus on the content of an attack rather than look at the attack in a broader context of how the attack will affect the functioning of the organization. Attacks masquerade as an attempt to correct mistakes, but the result is the disruption of the smooth functioning of an organization. Attention is deviated from the work of the organization to dealing with the attack. When a person approaches a leader with concerns, this can be helpful to the leader and an organization. The reason that this was an attack, as opposed to constructive criticism, was because (1) there had been no attempt to contact me to address the issues ahead of time to see if a resolution could be found, (2) it was a public way to discredit me and organize opposition to my leadership, and (3) its real purpose was not to correct any particular mistake that I had made, but to have me fired.

The meeting was adjourned and the board began to meet in a closed session to discuss my annual evaluation. In four years of operating the school, there had never been an evaluation of me in a closed meeting, but I was not worried about the outcome because I knew how hard I had been working as the principal and I naively expected everyone to behave in an above-board manner. As the meeting started, I realized that I had been set up. The chair of the Principal Evaluation Committee was Mr. V's wife. I realized too late what was happening. In my opinion, they operated as a team to discredit me. It must be said that at this point in our school we did not have a formal evaluation process for the principal and no documents had been given to me prior to this discussion, nor had anyone spoken to me about this evaluation beforehand. Mrs. V started off with a recitation of my shortcomings as the principal. After a few minutes, she stopped, turned to me, and said, "I don't know how much more you can take of this. Maybe you should leave and let the board discuss this privately." I indicated that I would stay. However, the board members, who were looking very uncomfortable at this point, agreed that I should go. That's when I made a big mistake. If I had not been blind-sided already and if I had had the fortitude that I gained over the next few years, I would have refused to go, but having already been severely shaken and not seeing a single ally in the room, I left.

I went straight to my office and called Terry Kant-Rauch, the former board chair who had been a supporter of mine for many years. I told her what was happening and cried a bucket of tears. I realized soon enough what a big mistake it had been to leave the room. In my absence, Mrs. V had the liberty to say whatever she wanted to and I never quite knew what she had said or what kind of damage had been done to my reputation in my absence. No one ever gave me a list of the accusations, so I never had the opportunity to share my side of the story or offer any evidence that was contrary to her accusations.

This was the first of a series of attacks on me during the next four years. I probably would have been bewildered and hurt by these attacks had I not previously led workshops on leadership and knew that leaders generally get attacked.

I spent the entire weekend writing and editing a long report to the board rebutting every point that had been made by Mr. V in his comments to the board. I included data to back up all of my responses, such as the results of parent and student attitude surveys that were overwhelmingly positive. I sent my report to all of the board members in an e-mail since they would not meet again for another month. I never got a chance to rebut what Mrs. V said because I wasn't present to hear it and did not receive any written communication regarding the issues that she had addressed.

My report was not discussed at the following board meeting. However, I was informed that the outcome of my evaluation was that the personnel committee would meet with me every month during the school year to track what I was doing as the principal. I was asked to write an action plan and report to them on my progress every month. Luckily for me, the board chair and the vice chair joined this committee and their intention was to figure out how to support me. Mrs. V and one of the school founders were also on the committee. Although she was not an actual founder, Mrs. V had been on the board since before I was hired as the principal. This made two original board members and two newer board members on this committee.

I believe that we are always free to choose our perspective. I must admit that I had to struggle a bit to find the right perspective for this situation, but I came up with it before the first meeting with the committee. I could have easily been resentful or hostile toward this committee. In my opinion I had worked hard to lead the school through many disasters and challenges and it felt insulting to be monitored so closely. However, at the beginning of that first meeting I told them that I was going to treat this committee like my support team; I would assume that its purpose was to help me become a better leader. The board chair and vice chair nodded their heads enthusiastically in agreement. Every month, I worked for hours on a report to that committee detailing what I had done that month and showcasing new initiatives that I was leading at the school. I was determined to win them over. Having learned a valuable lesson, I also worked on building my relationships with all of the board members, especially the new ones.

Several months later at the end of one of the committee meetings when I had shown them the new teacher evaluation process that I had developed with teacher input, everyone was picking up their things to leave and some were already out the door, when Mrs. V said: "She's a good old mule, but sometimes you have to hit her upside the head with a two-by-four to get her attention." I was shocked and walked into my office to regain my composure. When I walked out, she was sitting in the front office. I asked her to step into the conference room and told her behind a closed door that I did not appreciate what she had said. She shrugged it off by saying, "It's just an old southern saying." Her comment gave me a very clear picture of what she thought she was doing in regards to "this old mule."

In the spring, the evaluation committee decided that it would conduct interviews with teachers and staff to get their perspective on how I was doing my job. I was confident that the teachers would back me. Some weeks later, some of the teachers came to me to report that Mrs. V had told them that I was on probation that year and the board had someone "waiting in the wings" to take my place. All they needed was for the teachers to say negative things about me and I would be gone. Luckily, the committee was meeting a few days later, so I waited. When the meeting started, I reported what I had been told by a number of teachers. Jayme Harpring, the board vice chair was horrified. She turned to Mrs. V and asked, "Did you tell them that she was on probation?" "Yes, I did!" Mrs. V admitted, "Because I think she is!" The discussion that followed confirmed that I was not on probation and that Mrs. V was undermining my leadership and must stop. On a side note: we now have school policies that prohibit a board member from doing this sort of thing in the future.

Excerpt from the school's policy manual 2011:

Specific actions that are inappropriate for individual board members are:

1. Interfering with personnel issues. Individual board members must not be involved in personnel issues on campus other than as members of the board's personnel committee who will work as a group, not as individuals, to develop personnel policies.

2. Undermining the leadership of the principal. Board members must refrain from attacking, publicly criticizing, organizing against, or undermining the authority of the principal with students, parents, or staff members.

3. Directing the staff. Board members must refrain from directing office staff or teachers to do tasks that have not been approved by the principal in advance.

The teachers were supportive of my leadership. Some of them had read in e-mails that Mrs. V believed that they were too intimidated to talk to me about problems at the school. Because they knew that this was inaccurate and they wanted to set the record straight, teacher Ashley Arrington wrote a letter to the board that sixteen teachers signed in support of me and the school. "We are concerned with the comments to the board that address our alleged dissatisfaction with our work environment," they wrote. "We are satisfied with our jobs, our school, our board and our principal. There are times when we feel frustration, but we are lucky to have a community of supportive administrators, colleagues, parents and friends to carry us through." Mrs. V's response was that she didn't believe them. She later wrote: "Despite what Ashley's letter says, *I simply do not believe* (emphasis mine) that teachers have been free to express their frustrations, hopes and wishes, free from pressure from the top."

Having the support of the teachers helped me get through these difficult times. Despite the allegations of Mrs. V that the teachers were dissatisfied with how much input they had in the school, the exact opposite was true. We had created a school based on collaborative leadership and teacher empowerment. It was one of our greatest strengths. Details about how this worked at our school will be discussed further in chapters nine and eleven.

*****

We learned in our fifth year of operation that the US Department of Education's Office of Innovation and Improvement wanted to showcase a small group of outstanding charter schools from across the country. They were searching for the best examples and we were being considered in the top 150 schools. We were told that if we ended up in the top 15, someone would visit our school and make a report. If we were determined to be in the top eight, we would become one of the "rock stars" of the charter school movement. After working so hard to make our innovative school successful, we were pleased indeed. In January, a person did visit our school. She observed classrooms and talked to teachers, students, parents, board members, and administrators. She went back to California to write her report and submit it. All we could do was wait.

At the same time, the teachers were pushing again to drop from three grade levels per class to two in the elementary classrooms. They had approached the board to make the change at the end of the school's second year and were told that the school needed more time to develop before the board would consider such a major change to the school's charter. The teachers had acquiesced to the board's desires and continued to work as hard as they could for three more years to make the three-grade configuration work. The school had provided more opportunities for training to which the teachers eagerly responded. However, they had once more concluded that they could do better by the students with a two-grade configuration.

Meeting the needs of such a large range of student abilities and levels in one classroom with three grade levels was becoming even more difficult for teachers. As more parents learned about the school's successes and the student waiting list grew, the numbers of students with disabilities that were entering the school was increasing. Since we were an inclusion program, students with disabilities were in the same classrooms as regular students. This resulted in a wide range of abilities in every classroom. The teachers wanted every student to succeed and they thought that a two-grade classroom would be in the best interest of all the students.

Although the faculty reached a consensus opinion supporting the change to a two- grade configuration, there was one teacher who wanted to keep the three-grade configuration. Julie Fredrickson had been with the school from the beginning and she loved teaching third, fourth, and fifth grades in the same classroom. However, because of her support for the other teachers, she joined with the other teachers and "stood aside" on the vote. I, too, loved the three-grade configuration, but realized how hard the teachers were working to provide quality experiences in the classroom and how patient they had been about not pushing this issue for five years. During those five years, I had supported the teachers in every way that I could figure out in order to make the three-grade configuration work. Because we had a talented and diligent faculty who worked countless hours each week to make our thematic curriculum work, I trusted their assessment that they could do a better job for the students with a smaller span of ages in the multi-age classrooms. I knew that our school was successful because of these teachers and I thought that it was time to take the issue to the board again.

The board was in its own transition. After five years, some of the original founders were still on the board, but new people had been elected to the board over time. The board had started as a "founding board" which monitored the operations of the school to make sure that everything was on track. It was transitioning to a "professional board" which leaves the day-to-day operations of the school to the principal and the staff that she hires. Because of the board's own transitional stage, there were different perceptions and opinions about a major change to the charter design. While the founders held the charter design sacred, others thought that flexibility was in order. This clash between the original founders and the later board members is not atypical of what happens in many charter schools. The founders of the original charter have a vision that they hold to passionately. However, once that vision becomes a solid reality, there are inevitably changes that have to be made to fit the circumstances that were not conceived of originally. The beauty of charter schools is that they are flexible and adaptive to changing circumstances, but there is often a struggle with those who hold rigidly to the original ideas and are not willing to change as circumstances change.

The teachers made their case to the parent group and parents were divided on the issue also. Many parents had been involved in the school since the beginning and they wanted their children to remain in three-grade classrooms. They loved having their children in the same classroom with the same teacher for three years. Others thought that the teachers were right and their children's needs could be better served in a two-grade classroom. Many people were torn between liking the three-grade configuration and wanting to support the teachers. The teachers had such a high level of respect in the school community that many people trusted their thinking and backed them. It was an emotional time for the school and many people were adamant about their opinions being correct.

Change always causes upheaval. People tend to have a lot of feelings when things change. Knowing that these feelings are an inevitable part of change makes it easier to move forward. However, it is still a difficult process.

The board held a special meeting on the issue and organized it in a public meeting format. The meeting was held in the auditorium with the board sitting on the stage. There was a microphone on the floor level in the front of the rows of pews and anyone could come forward to address the board. I presented the teachers' proposal to the board and made a strong case for the change. After that, numerous people spoke—teachers, parents, and even students. After hearing everyone, the board had a discussion and voted. While most of the original founders voted against the teacher proposal, the majority on the board voted to support the teachers who were relieved by the positive vote. The board stipulated that the new grade configuration was an experiment that would last for one school year and be revisited by the board before the next year. However, after trying it for one year, there was no question that it would continue, although the board did revisit it as promised.

I believe that the grade configuration change was one more reason that a few very vocal people became dissatisfied with my leadership. The result of that split decision, which I presented on behalf of the teachers, made me the target of the fear that the school was not living up to the vision of the original charter and the founders were losing their power over its direction. That dissatisfaction was exemplified by repeated and unrelenting attacks upon me over the next few years, as well as a lawsuit against the board. These attacks were perpetrated by a few people. In all fairness, I believe that they perceived themselves as the only ones with the true picture of what the school should be, and in their eyes were trying to protect the school. However, based on my experience and my evaluation of the consequences, their tactics were usually based on stirring people up emotionally to gain support. Their actions undermined the school's progress by diverting the attention of the board and principal toward dealing with the attacks rather than working on legitimate school issues.

Ironically, just as this turmoil was beginning to brew, our school was named one of the top eight charter schools in the nation by the US Department of Education and was featured in a book entitled "Innovations in Education: Successful Charter Schools." This book is still available on the U.S. Department of Education's website. We were featured along with the other seven schools at the National Charter School Conference that summer. The principal from each of the eight schools spoke on two panels at the conference called

"School Leaders on Creating a Culture of Achievement" and "Walking the Talk: Leaders of 8 of the Nation's Most Successful Charter Schools." Each of the eight schools had a totally different philosophy and design. Someone listening to the panel commented to me later that the charter school movement was a "big tent" encompassing many different ideas and philosophies. I was proud that we were a part of it. One moment that stuck out to me at the National Conference was when US Secretary of Education Rod Paige mentioned our school by name in his keynote address and talked about our innovative curriculum.

Despite this accomplishment, there was trouble over my annual evaluation in the spring of 2004 after meeting monthly with the principal evaluation committee during the entire school year. When it was time for the committee to develop the final evaluation product, I was given a draft that only listed the ways that I needed to improve. I stated that I thought that an evaluation should state what the person had done well, as well as what needed improving. They agreed. Knowing that the committee members were too busy to rewrite the draft, I rewrote it myself. At the very top, I listed all of the recognitions that the school had received: one of the top eight charter schools in the nation and an "A" school based on FCAT scores. Following that, I made headings that stated what I was doing well and then, what I needed to work on. I included everything that had been listed in the original draft. Mrs. V was late for the meeting where I presented this and by the time she got there, this was the draft we were working with.

There were a few of the "needs to improve" that I wanted taken out because I could show that I had demonstrated competency in those areas. The committee agreed to take them out. Mrs. V said nothing. However, a week later, just one hour before the board meeting where the report would be presented, the board chair called me in tears. Mrs. V wanted those things added back into the document. If they were included, she wouldn't make a big scene at the board meeting. The board chair was very upset about contentiousness at the board meeting and, in support for her, I agreed to the changes and printed new copies for the meeting, even though I did not agree with the changes.

When the board discussed the evaluation, Mrs. V blasted me. The board vice chair was so angry by what Mrs. V was saying that they started yelling at each other. For the most part, I stayed quiet and let them argue over the details because it seemed to me that the board members were seeing for themselves what Mrs. V's tactics were. Eventually, after an emotionally strained meeting, the board approved the evaluation and the meeting was adjourned. Years later when Board Vice Chair Jayme Harpring completed her term on the board, she placed a letter in my personnel file describing what she considered inappropriate attacks on my leadership by Mrs. V. to ensure that there would be a record of what had transpired during this part of the school's history. Having allies like this reinforced my determination to keep going.

Following that contentious board meeting, I drove home to my little house located in a rural area outside of Tallahassee. Tucked away on three and a half acres of forest and gardens, this little cyprus-sided house was my refuge, my home, my retreat. I fled to the safety of my home.

I was so furious that I could hardly contain my anger. I felt like I had played fair. I had worked cooperatively with the committee and maintained a positive attitude. I had spent time in my busy schedule to prepare monthly reports to the committee about my activities. I had shown documentation that I had accomplished all of the goals that I had set. I had even been willing to revise the final evaluation document at the last minute in support of the board chair. On top of that, our school had been nationally recognized. And yet, I was still under attack.

I do not think that I have ever been that furious in my entire life, before or since. I was home alone and I do not have neighbors close-by. Knowing that there was no one who could hear me, I ranted and raved about the unfairness of this situation. The walls of my little house watched benignly and absorbed the assault of my words. Righteous indignation was followed by sobs and then, more righteous indignation. It was as if all of the frustration of the past few years came out in one loud roar. At the end of my 90 minute session, I felt purged and ready to continue as the principal of the school. I called a co-counselor to exchange listening time and continue to work through my anger and grief.

Attacks like this can bring up so many feelings for leaders that they either quit their job or continue under a load of discouragement. I was determined to do neither and purging my anger in an appropriate manner helped me to continue on with my head held high. Luckily for me, and the school, I am not a quitter. In many respects, I was "married" to this project and saw it as mine. It was an "until death do us part" kind of commitment for me, or at least "until retirement do us part." I knew that I served at the pleasure of the board and if they had asked me to quit, I would have complied. However, I refused to be driven out by attacks, no matter how unpleasant they were.

The only thing that ever caused me to consider quitting was when the board decided that they would change my contract from an eleven-month to a twelve-month commitment. This was actually a completely reasonable idea on the part of the board. A twelve-month contract is the norm for school principals, but I feared losing my summer recharging time in Montana. I knew that I would rather quit than give up my time in the wilderness that was so important to my well-being. Fortunately, the final negotiations on my contract resulted in enough vacation time that I would still get a month in Montana in the summer, but it would be paid time. This meant that if an emergency happened during the summer, I could be required to return in order to handle it. This was a win/win solution for everyone and I was grateful that the board had worked with me in order to arrive at this contract.

*****

We experienced progress in many areas in 2004-2005. Although we missed two school days in September due to hurricanes, there was no flooding or damage as a result of Hurricane Frances, nor subsequently of Hurricane Ivan. This was evidence that we had finally solved our flooding problems thanks to the work of a parent volunteer, Anthony Gaudio, who owned Apalachee Backhoe.

In the December 2004 issue of the newsletter "Dragon Times," I wrote: "*Sometimes it's easy to take it all for granted or to be disgruntled about some issue facing us, but when we step back a moment and take a look at how far we have come together, it is truly amazing.*"

Technology at our school took a major leap in the spring of 2005 due to a $97,375 grant from the Walton Family Foundation that I wrote. With this money, we were able to get laptops for every lead teacher and more computers for student use in every classroom. More classroom computers afforded students the ability to research information for their thematic projects and greatly improved our academic program. In addition, we installed a faster Internet connection and networked the entire school. Part of the story of our school is that we started with nothing and over the years developed a technologically advanced academic program by frugal management and attracting grants by being an excellent school.

However, other problems were brewing. In the spring of 2005, Mrs. V was up for re-election to the board. The board followed its usual procedure of asking the School Advisory Council (SAC) to interview the board candidates and make a recommendation to the board about who should be elected. The School Advisory Council consisted of equal representation of parents, teachers, and students. When SAC gave their list of nominees to the board for consideration, Mrs. V's name was not on the list. The board voted in April to elect the candidates recommended by the SAC.

Mrs. V objected to the process used to elect board members because it did not utilize a nominating committee made up of three board members and three SAC members as outlined in the charter and bylaws. She argued that the election should not stand. She also alleged that the SAC process violated the Government in the Sunshine Act (a law passed in 1976 intending to create more transparency in government, holding that "every portion of every meeting of an agency shall be open to public observation") because they did not keep minutes concerning their discussions about candidates and they met to interview candidates at times that were not noticed to the public.

The board reviewed her allegations at the May board meeting and agreed that the process had not occurred as specified in the charter and the bylaws. This is an example of an organization making a mistake by following a well-used process instead of referring back to original documents. The board realized its mistake and took action to correct it. They voted to void the election so that they could follow the process spelled out in the original documents. A nominating committee was created that consisted of three board members that would meet with three SAC representatives to go through the process from the beginning. They noted that any Sunshine violations made by an advisory council can be rectified by having the board take "final independent action in the Sunshine," according to legal precedent.

The new nominating committee began the process of developing a second set of recommendations to go to the board for the June board meeting. This included second interviews with all of the board candidates. The board is required to take the recommendations of the nominating committee into consideration, but is not bound to elect those recommended.

On May 31, 2005, Mrs. V's lawyer, Mr. V, filed a lawsuit against the school, naming all the board members, asking for damages in excess of $15,000 and alleging that the SAC was not representative of the school and therefore should not be allowed to participate in the election process. Board members were shocked that they were being sued when they were trying to remedy the situation that Mrs. V had brought to their attention. To make matters worse, even though the board had Director's and Officer's Insurance, they were informed by the insurance company that the expenses incurred by the lawsuit would not be covered because it was a case of one board member suing the others. The timing couldn't have been worse for Anthony Gaudio, parent and active volunteer who was now the board chair. Anthony was leaving on a three week vacation to Italy the following day. In Anthony's absence, the school obtained legal counsel to answer the lawsuit which required a response within twenty days from the date of filing. Although seeking mediation was considered by the board, the conditions for mediation presented by Mrs. V were deemed unacceptable. In the judgment of the board, her conditions for dropping the lawsuit and entering into mediation amounted to accepting her position as stated in the lawsuit before mediation began. The school's attorney filed a response before the deadline.

Prior to the June board meeting, Mr. V filed another motion asking for an immediate injunction to stop the election from proceeding. Judge Terry Lewis denied the motion stating, "There is no emergency here. There are no allegations that there is about to take place some meeting in violation of the Sunshine Law ..." The election proceeded as advertised. After considering the recommendations of the nominating committee, the board members voted independently and publicly on each candidate at the regular June board meeting. Mrs. V did not receive a single vote.

Although Mrs. V was right in pointing out the discrepancy between the school's election process and what was originally stated in the charter and bylaws, the board had quickly remedied this oversight. New election policies were written that mirrored the language in the charter and bylaws. The board had thrown out the first election and gone through the election process again to make sure that it was handled appropriately. The lawsuit was completely unnecessary in terms of fixing this problem. Since the mistake was corrected by the board, my conclusion is that this lawsuit was ultimately about power and control rather than correcting a mistake.

After the election, the lawsuit was still pending. Although the school felt that it was in an excellent position to defend against the allegations, it did not proceed due to the costs involved. The legal fees to defend against the lawsuit came from the school's operating budget and board members wanted to keep that expense to a minimum. Because neither party requested a hearing before a judge, the lawsuit was eventually dismissed. Not only did the lawsuit cost the school money, aggravation, and attention away from the school's mission, but there were individual consequences as well. For example, a member of the board who was an attorney moved to Tennessee and had to wait many months to be admitted to the Tennessee bar because of the pending lawsuit. In my opinion, the personal consequence for Mr. and Mrs. V was that they were viewed unfavorably by a large portion of the school population as a result of the lawsuit. Even though they ran for the board and SAC in years to come, neither was ever elected. For me, I was no longer the sole target of the attacks by Mr. and Mrs. V. This gave me many more allies who were committed to keeping our attention on moving the school forward.

*****

In the spring of that same school year, just one year after being recognized as one of the top eight charter schools in the nation, our school was named "a model school" by the International Center for Leadership in Education in conjunction with the Bill and Melinda Gates Foundation. After receiving this honor, I was asked to prepare a paper about our innovative curriculum to be published in the manual for the Model Schools Conference. Expenses were paid for four teachers and me to attend the Model Schools Conference at the Gaylord Opryland Hotel in Nashville, Tennessee. While there, I presented several workshops about our school. The timing was perfect because at the beginning of the school year, we had received a $100,000 Federal Dissemination Grant, the purpose of which was to disseminate our best practices to a wide range of educators. With the grant money, we bought video equipment for every classroom and started recording our students and teachers at work. A group of teachers (Eden Rush, Brandon Alexander, Eirin Lombardo, Ashley Arrington, and Corey Collins) edited the material and created a 20-minute video about our school that was sent to educators all over the country. The video's debut was at the Model Schools Conference. The school was moving forward despite the lawsuit.

As a result of our school's excellence, I was asked to serve on the national Task Force for Charter School Quality and Accountability in 2005 sponsored by the National Alliance for Public Charter Schools. Members of the task force met in four locations (Washington D.C., Chicago, New Haven, and Denver) over the next year to observe quality charter schools and write a report. The report can be found on the website for the National Alliance for Public Charter Schools. As a result of serving on this task force, I gained a wider perspective on the charter school movement nationwide and brought back many good ideas to our school. I began to see our school as not only a local experiment in quality education but as a major player on the national stage of the charter school movement.

In the October 2005 "Dragon Times," I wrote:

Our school keeps getting recognized as an excellent school.

What is excellence?

Excellence is more than good test scores. Excellence is the excitement in a child's eye when she walks across the crosswalk on her way to class in the morning. Excellence is the quality performance by a child who was once too shy to speak above a whisper. Excellence is the joy of discovery when a child grasps a new concept. Excellence is the animated discussion of a group of teachers sitting around a table sharing their newest classroom ideas. Excellence is a friendly voice on the phone thanking you for calling the school. Excellence

is a parent finding time after a long day to read to his
child. Excellence is a diverse school community that
abounds with respect for everyone.

Achieving excellence in a school takes the energy
and commitment of every teacher, parent, student, board
member, and administrator. Join us in creating excellence
at SAS!

During that year, I was also appointed by the Speaker of the Florida House of Representatives to serve on the Charter School Review Panel, which reviews and suggests legislation regarding charter schools. I served in this capacity for two years. The Florida Commissioner of Education also asked me to serve on the Charter School Appeals Commission which hears cases involving districts and charter schools and makes recommendations to the Florida Board of Education regarding the outcome. I served on the commission for six years until my retirement as principal and was re-appointed to it a few years later. Once again, these opportunities gave me the chance to be intimately involved in the charter school movement in Florida.

*****

During the 2005-2006 school year, the attacks picked up again. Before starting the School of Arts and Sciences, I had witnessed attacks in many organizations in which I had been involved, but this was the first time that they had been so persistently aimed at me. In all of my previous experience in other organizations, my leadership had ushered in a period of peace that had previously been contentious. However, whatever I was doing this time just brought on more attacks. It was difficult not to be bewildered by them. I knew that I was committed to the school and working hard for its vision. I knew that my intentions were good and that I was always trying to do the right thing, so I couldn't understand how some people could become so confused about me. Over time, I developed a thicker skin.

From the very first day of the first school year, our teachers and staff had been working hard to create an environment of peace and respect on campus. We started with ourselves by pledging to speak directly to each other when we had conflicts rather than resort to gossip and criticism behind each other's back. This pledge was a reminder of our commitment to each other and it worked extremely well to keep us working cooperatively as a team. During the 2005-2006 pre-planning week, the teachers suggested that we invite the parents to join us in the pledge. This information was sent home to parents during the first week of school.

Our intention was to extend and solidify our culture of respect and invite the parents to join with us. However, Mr. V used a parent e-mail list to claim that I was trying to stifle dissent and that it was everyone's right in a democratic society to criticize people in leadership in order to avoid tyranny. It is interesting to me that this fear was raised in a school that provided so many avenues for people to participate, express their opinions, and be heard by the board and administration.

Mr. V had obtained the parent e-mail list when I mistakenly forgot to use the blind carbon copy feature in an e-mail to school members. My mistake allowed parents to get the e-mail addresses of many of the other parents. Lyn Kittle, who usually managed the school e-mail list, later sent a follow-up e-mail asking parents not to use the e-mail addresses. "Our policy is that this list is confidential and not to be used as a group mailing list for anything other than official school e-mails," she wrote. Mr. V ignored this policy and sent out his mass e-mail. The same day, Lyn e-mailed parents again reminding them about the policy. Two days later, Mr. V sent out a mass e-mail saying that parents could request to be off his e-mail list, but he didn't agree to stop using it. Although I felt like kicking myself for making this mistake, there wasn't anything else that we could do about it besides just let it play out.

Several parents who received the e-mail messages responded to Mr. V asking that he not use school e-mail to engage in attacks on the school's respectful environment and to take their names off his list. A few of them engaged in a series of back-and-forth exchanges with him, but became frustrated and decided to stop trying to communicate. Eventually, his attack lost momentum.

Knowing that people would stand up for me gave me courage and determination to keep going despite anything that was said about me. Dr. Martin Luther King said that what hurts the most is "not the words of our enemies, but the silence of our friends." It was gratifying that my friends were not silent.

The school year continued with everyone on staff feeling like we had made great progress in solidifying our curriculum. Our successes had been validated, honored, and publicized on a national level and we were excited to push forward as we learned new things about educating children in an innovative learning environment. We were focused on continuing to make the school the best that it could be. However, an incident occurred in February of 2006 that caused more upset.

Even in a school with a respectful culture like ours, sometimes children did things that were highly inappropriate. When these things happened, we followed the policies that had been approved by the board in terms of consequences for the young person who was acting out, but we also applied attention, counseling, and compassion to that young person as well as to the young people who were the targets of the misbehavior. I had prior experience in teaching classes on listening skills and peer counseling techniques for both adults and young people, so I brought those skills into my job as principal. Since we did not have a guidance counselor on staff, I often spent many hours a day listening to young people and helping them work through their difficulties. While it was obvious that we needed a counselor on staff, our tight budget did not allow for this. The result was that I worked extra time every day to make up for the hours I spent listening to young people. Even so, counseling young people did not get the attention it deserved because of all my other responsibilities in running a school.

In our school, if a student's behavior could not be dealt with through the normal classroom procedures, the teacher would write an incident report and send the student to me. This did not happen very often, but when it did, it was usually the result of physical or verbal conflict between two students. I served in the role of mediator or counselor whenever these things occurred. Students who used actual physical violence were suspended. This meant that their parents were called and they went home for the rest of the day. While waiting for the parents to come pick up a young person, I had time for further counseling. My belief is that no one would ever harm another person unless they had been hurt previously and were acting out that hurt on someone else. The hope was that the young person could heal from the hurt and not continue to pass on the hurtful behavior in the future. Our discipline procedures have always been more focused on healing the hurts and changing the behavior rather than just punishment.

In February of 2006, I received an incident report from a teacher which stated that a second grade boy in her classroom had put his hand down the back of a second grade girl's pants and grabbed her bottom. He was sent to me. I dropped what I was doing and immediately met with him to begin counseling. He was a very small boy and although I couldn't get him to say much, I sensed that he was frightened and unaware that what he had done was inappropriate. My assumption was that he had witnessed two consenting adults doing this and it seemed like a fun thing to do. I explained to him that this was called sexual harassment and was not a respectful thing to do. His parents were called to pick him up from school. When they arrived, I met with them to discuss the incident. They were completely cooperative and apologetic for their son's behavior. This is not always the case with parents. In my experience, in similar cases, many parents become belligerent and deny that their child did anything wrong. These particular parents were concerned and supported the school's consequences for the behavior. They assured me that they would instruct their son about proper conduct toward girls.

I had met with the girl who was involved in this incident. She explained what had happened. I was thinking that this was an isolated incident. However, this girl later spoke to several of her girlfriends about the incident and several admitted to her that it had happened to them too. A few days later, they came to see me to tell me their stories. All of their stories matched in the details. The boy had slipped his hand into the back of their pants and grabbed their bottoms. They had been embarrassed and confused by the incident and had never told anyone. We talked about unwanted and inappropriate touching and how this should always be reported to an adult. The girls told their parents and there was a considerable amount of upset around these incidents.

Because I now had evidence that the boy had a pattern of repeated misbehavior of this type, the issue needed to be handled in a different way. I talked to the boy once more, but he wouldn't say much about what had happened, what his intentions had been, where he had gotten the idea to grab girls' behinds, or if that had ever happened to him. He just seemed tiny and scared to me. I called his parents into my office for a second discussion. Moving him to another classroom was not a good option. The only other second/third grade classroom was next door to his and the two groups interacted regularly. This would not create enough separation, so I asked his parents to withdraw their son from our school. It was obvious to me that there was so much upset around the issue that it was interfering with the learning process in the classroom and that the girls were very uncomfortable around him now that they had started talking to each other about what had happened to them. His parents agreed to enroll him in their neighborhood public school. In my opinion, he had learned from this experience and would not be acting out in this way again. However, I encouraged them to seek further counseling for him. At no time did I see him as a sexual predator or a person who was a threat to other children. I saw him as a very young (seven-year-old) male child who had started doing something that he was not aware was inappropriate. Now that he knew, I did not think it would continue. However, his pattern of behavior had ruined his chance to be accepted as a trusted member in his classroom by his classmates for the foreseeable future. It seemed to me that it was in the best interest of everyone that he had a new start in a completely new situation.

The girls continued to come to my office most days to talk about what had happened. They would ask their teacher if they could come to see me and she would let them. Whenever they came by, I always made time for them. They seemed very relieved that the boy was gone, although they sometimes saw him in his parents' car at the end of the school day at the car pick-up spot because he still had siblings at the school. This bothered them and we talked about their feelings. Before long, the boy's family withdrew all of their children from the school. In my opinion, the girls were doing fine and working through their feelings about what had happened. Everything seemed like it was getting back to normal and the issue had been resolved. I was wrong. Although the young people were working through the issue, their mothers were on a different track.

Many of the mothers blamed the classroom teacher for not catching the misconduct earlier. Defending this teacher was easy for me. She was an exemplary teacher who had been at the school from the beginning. Her classroom was one of the most organized and peaceful classrooms in the school. She always talked to her students in a calm, quiet voice and the students followed her model. In addition, she had a reputation for being able to work with the most rambunctious boys and keep them focused on productive things. I knew that she would never knowingly allow students to hurt other students and felt that she should not be held responsible for something of which she had not been aware.

The mothers were furious with me that the boy had not been expelled from the school. They claimed that this behavior had been going on for years and that we had overlooked it. I searched our records and found no evidence of any incident reports prior to the one that initiated our response. I was told by parents that the boy had done a similar thing to a girl in the first grade, but there was no record of it and the teacher was no longer at our school. I called the teacher in California and determined that this had in fact happened, but no incident form had been filled out. Another mother reported that the boy had exposed himself to her son in the first grade, but there was no record of this either because it was not witnessed by a teacher. Mrs. V became the ringleader of the irate mothers.

As the mother of a daughter myself, I had compassion for these mothers. They were worried about the effect of these incidents on their daughters. I met with them and listened to their concerns. They were clearly very upset and used language like "sexual perpetrator" and the "perp" when referring to the seven-year-old boy. I agreed to hire a counselor to work with the children and investigate the situation.

The counselor met with the children individually and in a group. After interviewing eight students, he determined that seven—six girls and one boy were involved. The students asked that I be present for the group meeting since they had been talking to me all along. I attended as a listener and I heard all of the same things that had been told to me by these students in earlier meetings.

The counselor met with the parents and reported to me that the parents were going to ask the board to fire the teacher and me because they felt that we had not handled the situation properly. He recommended to them that, in the best interest of the children, they should not do this. He pointed out that the children had expressed their caring for their teacher and the principal and that it would detrimentally affect them if they thought that speaking out had caused people who they cared about to be fired. This did not deter the parents from this action.

One hour before the March board meeting, a newscaster from a local television station called to ask if our board meetings were open to the public. I assured them that as a public school our board meetings were open to the public. They said that they would be there to report on the issue. I asked them why they would consider this newsworthy. They told me that when a group of parents were calling for the firing of a principal, that this was news. I called the board chair, Anthony Gaudio, to make sure that he knew that the television news media would be present at the meeting. We would not have known that this was going to happen if the station had not called prior to the meeting. However, there was no time to alert the rest of the board who were surprised when they arrived.

The classroom where the board meeting was held each month was like a three-ring circus that night. The place was packed with people, the majority of whom were teachers who had come to support the teacher and me, but on the television news it looked like they were all irate parents. Two television stations were there with all of their bright lights and intimidating presence. The room was filled with tension and nervous energy. Mrs. V had hired a court reporter with her own funds to record everything from the meeting. The unspoken message to the board was that they were in danger of another lawsuit.

I presented my report to the board under the lights of the television cameras in as calm a way as I could under the strain. I presented the sequence of events, outlined school policy, and listed what the school had done and was doing to address the issue. Mrs. V addressed the board and spoke of sexual abuse of children. I looked at her directly during her entire presentation, but I must admit that she succeeded in intimidating me. I was scared and confused. Sexual abuse? I started to question myself. These were same-age peers, seven-year olds. I had always thought of sexual abuse as someone bigger, stronger, or older using their power over someone in a sexual way. I had been dealing with this situation as sexual harassment. Was I wrong? Several parents spoke and one asked the board to fire the principal and the teacher. Several teachers spoke in support of us.

The board decided to have the personnel committee review how the staff had handled the issue and make a recommendation to them at the next board meeting. They also formed a committee made of board members and parents to review the school policies and recommend any changes needed.

I was pretty shaken up and wanted to just run away after the board meeting, but I had to make a statement for the news station who had called me earlier. I disappeared into the bathroom to compose my thoughts. Susan Parks, a board member, went with me for encouragement and support. Terrified does not adequately convey how I felt at that moment. I was more scared than at any point during my entire tenure as principal; I was shaking and so scared that I couldn't think. I had no idea what to say to the news camera. Mrs. V had completely confused me with her talk of sexual abuse. I was still reeling from her words and doubting myself. I knew that I had tried to do the right thing—for everyone involved, but it was terrifying to think that maybe I had made a big mistake. "Come on, Debo," I said to myself, "Get it together. You have to see this though. Too many people are counting on you." Minutes were ticking by and I had to make an appearance. Susan's supportive attention helped as I shook and talked out loud about what I would say. Then, I went to talk to the reporters.

When I see cameras and microphones shoved into the faces of leaders during stressful situations, I have a great deal of sympathy for them because I know what that kind of pressure feels like. I cannot recall exactly what I said to the reporters, although I know that I kept the message positive and outlined how the school had handled the situation. The television station that called me prior to the meeting was the one that acted responsibly and interviewed many different people, including me, for their story. The other news station only interviewed Mrs. V and presented the story with the most inflammatory words possible. The catchy line to get people to watch the eleven o'clock news that night was something like: *Sexual predator is allowed to run rampant on campus while the principal and the teacher turn a blind eye...*

We were stunned by the negative publicity. We wanted to respond and defend ourselves, but someone with news experience recommended that we not respond in any way and just let it go. They said, "The public has a short attention span. Just let it fade away in people's minds." That was good advice although it was difficult to just sit back and let our good reputation be tarnished.

I was later told by one of the mothers in the parent group that they had no idea that someone was going to call the news media. They were just as surprised as we were and hated the negative publicity that the school received. She also said that not everyone in the group agreed with all of the group's recommendations, such as the firing of the teacher and principal, but they went along in order to have a united front. In my opinion, Mrs. V took the very legitimate concerns of these parents and inflamed the situation to support her personal vendetta against me.

One member of the audience during that contentious board meeting was Dr. Iris Palazesi, a visitor to the school, attending the meeting to find out how the board operated. She was considering becoming involved in the school by running for election to the board. After witnessing that evening, it is a wonder that she persisted, but Iris is not one to turn away from trouble. She later became one of our longest serving board members and was the chair of the board for three of those years. When I asked her many years later why she didn't just run away after that dramatic meeting, she replied that it showed her that she was needed. We were fortunate to be able to attract many courageous leaders throughout the school's history.

We were very busy for the next month dealing with the aftermath of the meeting. Many good things came out of it. The counselor's report stated that he had found no symptoms of emotional trauma in the children and that they felt safe at school and had good relationships with their teacher and principal. I wrote a report for the personnel committee detailing everything that we had done and they reported to the board that we had followed all of the school policies in dealing with the issue. They recommended that the principal and the teacher not be fired as requested by the group of parents. We began a training program for teachers on how to discuss good touch/bad touch issues with their students in age-appropriate ways. I worked with the policy committee to draft a new policy that more clearly spelled out the procedures for dealing with sexual misconduct. The board passed this policy the following month. I also found room in the budget for a part-time guidance counselor to be hired for the following school year.

After the news coverage, the charter school liaison with Leon County Schools was furious with me about not informing the district about the issues associated with the second grade boy that enrolled in one of their schools. She was right. I should have notified them. I should have called the principal. I explained to her the situation, my assessment, and how cooperative the family had been. She calmed down and forgave me, although she stated that if we had expelled him, there would have been a process for getting him back into a public school. I also apologized to the principal of the school where the boy and his siblings enrolled and explained the situation to her. As far as I know, things have worked out fine there.

Any issues around sex are always charged with emotional distress and navigating through those feelings requires skill and calmness in the face of upset. There was a great deal of distress around this issue, including many unsubstantiated rumors about the nature of what had happened that fueled feelings to a fever pitch. While I did the best I could to handle this situation, it became clear to me that there were some things that needed to be improved. The use and tracking of incident reports was a case in point. If we had recorded and been able to see a pattern of behavior earlier, we could have intervened before it affected so many children. We might have been able to help this young boy before his behavior escalated and he became a target of many people's wrath. In addition, we needed to work on empowering our students, particularly the female students, to speak out when inappropriate behavior was occurring.

One question that we were left to grapple with concerned the difference between sexual harassment and sexual abuse. Bev Owens, our charter school liaison with Leon County Schools (LCS), asked LCS attorney Jeff Whalen to take a look at our newly revised policy on sexual misconduct. Because of issues raised at our school about the proper way to deal with sexual harassment, Jeff studied the issue and determined that school administrators throughout the county had not been adequately informed about the kinds of incidents that should be reported to the Department of Children and Families (DCF). In a PowerPoint presentation given at the LCS Principal's Meeting on August 16 that I attended, he stated that while everyone had been diligent about reporting adult on child abuse, there were instances where it would be required that school officials report child on child abuse to DCF as well. He clearly stated that if school personnel witness child on child abusive behavior, it must be reported so that DCF can investigate the home situation of the perpetrating student to determine if that child is acting out behaviors that are happening to him or her. Severe incidents must also be reported to the sheriff's department to determine if criminal charges are needed. This information, explained at a public meeting, clarified for me and other principals how certain issues should be handled in the future. I used Jeff's

PowerPoint presentation to inform our teaching staff about these issues. This is one more example of the ways in which our charter school worked cooperatively with the school district.

In the April 2006 "Dragon Times," I wrote:

The founders of this school wrote a mission statement that included the words: "safe and nurturing environment." This is one of our highest ideals as a school community. We created this kind of environment from the start, but we have to be continually vigilant to maintain it.

Having a safe environment does not mean that nothing will ever go wrong or that no one will ever make a mistake, but it does mean that we have a consciousness about this; that we strive to create it in every interaction that we have with another person. It means that we as adults model for the young people kindness and cooperation. It means that we strive to act on our best thinking rather than our painful emotion. It means that we create a place where love is stronger than hate and trust is stronger than suspicion. It is a place where we notice the best intentions in others; a place where we can forgive mistakes and help each other grow.

Our school is a special place. We are a family. At times we have disagreements. At times we are not at our best. But we have times when we notice our connection to each other and the extraordinary school that we have built.

It is important to always remember that every person in our school is working hard to create and maintain a safe and nurturing environment for our children. It is the most important part of our mission.

Despite all of the drama during these transition years, it was not a big surprise to us that the Leon County School Board renewed our charter for another five years in the spring of 2006. Although we asked for a 15-year renewal, we were told that the district wanted to keep all of their charter schools on a 5-year renewal schedule.

*****

We began the 2006-2007 school year with a part-time school counselor. She immediately began to develop a guidance program for the school and her position grew to full-time in later years. I was particularly happy with this addition because we now had someone whose main job was to focus on the emotional well-being of the students and staff. Cathryn Lokey built close relationships with the students and teachers and started teaching weekly guidance lessons in all classrooms. Our respectful learning environment reached new heights under her enthusiastic leadership.

We continued to receive recognition as an outstanding school. In November, our school was recognized at the Florida Charter School Conference as one of the excellent charter schools in the state. Ten schools received this recognition and were included in a publication by the Florida Department of Education called "A Decade of Progress" celebrating ten years of charter schools in Florida.

At that state conference, Bev Owens, our LCS Charter School Liaison, and I led a workshop called "Building a Good Relationship between the Charter School and the District." Judging from the amount of conflict between charter schools and districts throughout the state, this workshop offered a hopeful perspective for many.

Technology continued to improve at our school. Mark Baldino, a board member who worked for IBM, ensured that we received a grant for new IBM computers each year for several years. As an IBM employee, he could purchase the computer equipment for one-fifth of the cost which was donated to the school. In addition, the Walton Family Foundation awarded our school with a follow-up grant for $132,625 which we used to place smart boards in every classroom serving grades second through eighth grade and purchase more student and teacher computers.

In the spring of 2007, Carlo Rodriguez, the director of the School Choice Office at the Florida Department of Education, lobbied me to accept the job of director of charter schools in his office. He encouraged me to use my leadership skills to benefit the entire charter school movement in the state. The offer caught me by surprise and I was very flattered and excited to be asked to do this important job. Because I find new challenges and leadership opportunities compelling, I thought, at first, that there was no way that I could justify not taking this obvious promotion and ascension into the charter school limelight. The salary and benefits were better than my current position and the chance to influence the direction of charter schools in Florida was very enticing. However, there were many factors that caused me to turn down the job.

The most important reason for refusing the job offer was my commitment to my school. I firmly believe that a leader should prepare the way for the next leader before abandoning an important project. In addition, I would only be allowed to continue working for five years under the Florida Retirement Service's DROP program after I had thirty years of service in the public educational system. I had a lot to do to prepare my school for a transition to a new leader and I felt like the charter school movement needed a longer commitment than I would be able to give. There were personal issues as well. The idea of leaving behind my beautiful school campus and the happy smiles and hugs of children saddened me. In addition, the idea of working in a windowless office in a 17-story office building felt claustrophobic to an outdoors person like me, especially when compared to my present office with its glass door to the green outside world and the bank of windows overlooking the school garden. To move from the relative autonomy of running my own school to being "a suit" in a huge state bureaucracy was both fascinating and repulsive to me and I feared that it would not fill me with the kind of joy that I felt every day at the School of Arts and Sciences. Although the director job offered significant vacation time, I doubted that I would be allowed to take a whole month each summer to continue my construction projects in Montana. For many reasons, I decided to remain the principal until I retired. It is interesting to me to recall that even though the transition years were my most difficult years as principal, I did not accept a great job offer that would have given me a graceful escape.

The transition years of our school were filled with drama and conflict, as well as national and state recognition as an outstanding charter school. Through all of the challenges, we persisted in offering an extraordinary academic program in a respectful, innovative learning environment. Through all the turmoil of these years, we kept our eyes on the mission and moved forward.

As a result of our excellent reputation and our high test scores, our lottery pool continued to grow during the transition years and was more than double the population of the school. People were clamoring to be part of what we were doing. It is interesting to note that while a few unhappy people were attempting to denigrate the course that the school was taking, our school had in fact become a "rock star" in the charter school movement.

Chapter 4: The Maturing Years 2007-2011

The honeymoon years may be the most exciting and hopeful and the transition years may be the most tumultuous, but the maturing years are definitely the most satisfying. There comes a time in the development of an organization, or relationship, that the power struggles lessen and the members begin to work toward something that is bigger than themselves. They can set aside their own needs for the bigger picture, the greater good. This is the most constructive period for an organization.

As a charter school, we had truly discovered ourselves. We knew who we were and what we were about. The early insecurities and doubts were behind us. This period was characterized by a board of directors that had matured and become a professional board, aware of the differences between its role and the role of the principal. The board became a truly working board with active committees who accomplished things and reported back at board meetings. The board began to think about not only the current year's issues but also what lay ahead for the school. It began to organize a strategic planning process and set goals for the future.

The board had become very cohesive and had learned from experience how to handle attacks. Having been the target of a frivolous lawsuit, they had become savvy about recognizing things that attempted to pull their attention away from the school's mission. In addition, they had figured out how to support me. The final attack against me came in the form of an e-mail from Mr. V to a large group of parents. This was followed by a seven page letter to me ranting that my involvement in a peer counseling organization outside of school and my ideas about listening to each other were corrupting the school. We had learned from hard experience that to address any of his issues or to try to show evidence to prove that the allegations were incorrect only brought on more vitriol from him. Our stance became, "Don't give him any juice," and so I simply replied "Thanks for the input." My short, non-combative response must have angered him because he sent a three-page letter to every board member with the seven-page letter to me attached. One of the board members approached him and asked why he kept his children at the school if he truly believed the things that he had written. He replied that this was the best school for his children.

"Persons to be Heard" is always the last item on the board agenda. The board chair, Susan Parks, recognized Mr. V and told him that he had three minutes to speak. In his speech, Mr. V started painting a dismal picture of what was happening at the school and my negative influence on it. He ended by threatening that if the board did not hold a public meeting for the community to discuss his allegations that he would take it to the Leon County School Board. When he finished, the board chair thanked him for his input. Rather than asking for comments, she turned to the board and said, "I'll entertain a motion to adjourn." There was a motion, a second, and the meeting was adjourned. People started eating brownies and talking pleasantly with each other. Mr. V looked amazed that his comments had not generated a flurry of discussion. He quickly walked out the door. That was the last trouble he caused. This event marked the end of the years of turmoil and transition for the school. It was the signal that we had matured as a school and had become confident about what we were doing.

Mr. and Mrs. V had three wonderful children who attended our school. These children took leadership roles within the school in a variety of ways and were real assets to our program. I never lost sight of the fact that Mr. and Mrs. V were good people who cared deeply about the school and contributed in many ways to its success despite the series of attacks that they launched at me. Throughout the conflicts, I continued to treat them with respect and friendliness despite how hurtful some of their actions were. I suppose that one of the feisty female protagonists in the mystery novels that I love to read would have aggressively confronted Mr. and Mrs. V, but my natural inclination is to work collaboratively and my philosophy about human beings allowed me to see the good in them despite their behavior toward me. While some may see this as weakness, I agree with Mahatma Gandhi that "we must be the change that we seek in the world."

After many years of operating a charter school, I had matured as principal and my accumulation of experience and thinking was obvious in the day-to-day operations. There were still issues, of course, but these were handled with a confidence and self-assurance that comes from having survived various struggles at the school and learned many things from them. The demonstration of the board's total support in response to the final attack on me gave me a buoyancy and sureness that positively affected everything that I did from then on. The understandable tension that I previously had before board meetings had dissipated and I began to look forward to them. The school was in better shape than ever before and I was energized as its leader. Although I was again approached to accept the job at the state charter school office, I was clear that my path would continue at the School of Arts and Sciences.

I had finally settled into a work routine that was both healthy and productive. Things that I had given up in order to focus on the school were open to me again. I was taking much better care of myself by finding the time for exercise, cooking healthy food, and not missing my weekly co-counseling sessions. Dancing also contributed to my well-being. I found that after being deeply engrossed mentally all day at school, I needed engaging physical activity after work. Since my daughter had graduated from high school and was no longer living with me, I went to dance classes several nights a week. I practiced with a partner and competed in national dance competitions. The mind/body connection of dance was like a healing salve after a busy work day. I had time again for gardening and began to grow camellias and citrus trees in my yard. My idea was to grow things that produce flowers and fruits in the winter because I planned to be in Montana for six months each year once I retired. I continued to spend summer vacations in Montana working on my cabin which eventually had both solar electricity and running water.

The school accomplished much during this phase of development. One of the most notable was the construction of a new building. It had taken five years to get through the permitting process because of neighborhood opposition that culminated in a hearing before an administrative judge. The city attorneys had spoken for us at the hearing and we persevered. The judge ruled in our favor and now the way was clear for us to move forward. We had been putting money into a reserve fund for years and this frugal management gave us the leverage to re-finance our school property in order to fund the new construction.

Some of the younger students cried when a few big pine trees had to be cut down to make way for the new building, but shortly afterward the student council held a "ground breaking" ceremony and turned over the first shovelfuls of dirt. It was disruptive, exciting, and educational to live in a construction zone and watch the building go up. Thanks to the efforts of two board members, Anthony Gaudio and Bob Goodwin, who worked tirelessly on the project and Rippee Construction, who managed the project, the building was finished just in time for the opening of school in 2008. It was a beautiful building, designed to match the architecture of the adjoining building, and housed two middle school classrooms and a future media center.

Along with approval for the new building, we were finally able to make adjustments in our traffic flow as well. With the new design plan, car traffic could enter and exit the campus from the main entrance without traveling through the neighborhood. This helped to alleviate tension with the neighborhood, although the school buses continued to exit through the neighborhood because there was not enough space on campus for them to turn around.

During this period, our auditorium also took a major step forward. When we first purchased our property, we turned the church's sanctuary into an auditorium that included a stage with a beautiful wooden floor installed with voluntary parent labor. However, during our maturing years, the stage became an actual theatrical stage rather than just a raised platform. Lyn Kittle saw some beautiful royal blue stage curtains being thrown away at a Leon County School that was getting a new curtain. She asked if she could have the curtain and arranged to get it to our school. Even in the later years of our school, we were still scavenging to get things that we could not afford new. After some adjustments and several volunteers from the Tallahassee theatre community who knew how to hang the curtain, we now had a professional-looking stage with a curtain that could be closed and opened during performances. In addition, teachers voted to use some of our school improvement money on stage lighting. These improvements not only enhanced our performing arts curriculum, but improved the quality of our Friday Sing programs.

Large budget cuts due to the economic recession kept us from accomplishing everything that we wanted to do during those years. However, due to wise financial management and President Obama's stimulus dollars in 2009 and 2010, we avoided having to decrease our teaching staff. One of the causalities of "The Great Recession" was our media center. Although we dreamed of having a space equipped with all kinds of technology that would provide opportunities for student research and production, it was determined each year that it made more financial sense to put a classroom in the room designated for the media center. In that way, we would be bringing in more state funding for the additional students and foregoing the expense of setting up a media center and paying a media specialist. Even though this was a good decision financially, it was heart-breaking to put off this dream every year.

Another casualty of the recession was our real life science program that had been operating for a number of years funded by a combination of grants from the Rintels Foundation and expenditures from the school budget. Developed and operated by Carolyn Schultz, this program was exceptional in bringing hands-on science to the elementary classrooms. However, because it was a supplemental program, we did not have the resources to both support the program and balance our budget. Parents worked extraordinarily hard to keep this program alive through fundraisers, personal contributions, and finding donors. One parent in particular, Jenny Maddox, was named the Tallahassee Volunteer of the Year for her efforts to raise money for the Real Life Science Program. In the end, fundraising could not sustain the program and it had to be downgraded to a part-time program. However, it remains a hands-on science program that is an integral part of the elementary curriculum.

*****

In 2008, we applied to become an accredited school with the Southern Association of Colleges and Schools (SACS). The process of receiving accreditation entails school improvement planning. There are eight areas that the applying school must address. We divided the areas among groups who would assess the school's progress. I worked with each group and took notes on the ideas that they brainstormed. I then took their ideas and wrote a draft that went back to the group for suggestions and additions. The final report captured the thinking of everybody in the school who wanted to be involved. Although the visiting team who came to our campus to write an assessment knew very little about charter schools, they produced a good report and recommended that we be accredited. This recommendation was approved and we were proud to be the first charter school in Leon County to become accredited.

All public schools were suffering from budget cuts, and the Leon County school district was no exception. To save money, they decided to stop providing bus transportation for charter schools. Instead, they offered to give us a few of their surplus buses to operate ourselves. We would develop bus routes and protocols, hire and supervise drivers, and deal with parent issues. In turn, they would provide maintenance, parking, and fuel at cost. At first, this seemed like a massive setback for us. We worried that it would cost us too much money and increase the workload of an already-overworked office staff. However, it turned out to be cost effective and much more convenient for field trips and early release days because we could make our own schedules rather than conform to the district's schedule. In addition, we had buses with our school name on them!

Our parent organization, under the leadership of some very good presidents, helped to raise money and organize the parents for some huge projects that increased the effectiveness of our educational program and the safety of our campus. Jenny Maddox, a parent volunteer, brought her considerable talent to school fundraising. She and other parents organized an annual family Valentine's dance on a Sunday afternoon that usually included a live band, games for the children, a silent auction, and food. The children loved playing and dancing with the adults. Not only was it a huge community building event, but it raised a lot of money for projects. The most ambitious project was the installation of new playground equipment in the lower playground. The parents raised money and spent several weekends building a wooden ramp that provided an accessible path from the office level of the campus to the lower playground and the kindergarten and first grade classrooms. This ramp contained many opportunities for play and adventure along its path, including slides, climbers, and play areas. It was amazing to see how many parents showed up on weekends to help build the ramp and I enjoyed wielding a hammer or a drill alongside the parents. In addition, the parents added a fence that separated the campus from busy Thomasville Road and moved a gazebo to campus for an outdoor classroom for the gardening classes. Over the years, parents had been instrumental in helping to develop the campus, but it was especially evident during our maturing years.

Our charter was scheduled for renewal in spring 2011. Before this time, the charter renewal process entailed attending a Leon County School Board meeting and making a short report followed by a board vote to approve the renewal for five years. Now, Leon County had five charter schools and they had developed a much more stringent process. Schools requesting renewal had to write a large report with charts and graphs covering many different areas of accountability. The model report that we were given as a guide to writing our report was from another district in Florida. Rather than be upset by the tremendous amount of work involved in writing the report, I decided that the goal was to write such a good report that in the future the district would use our report as the model. I asked for the help of various members of our staff to compile the data for the report and the final product was exemplary. The report requested a fifteen-year charter renewal rather than the typical five-year renewal. Florida state law said that a high performing charter school could receive a fifteen-year renewal if they were an "A" or "B" school and had an outstanding financial situation. We met both of the criteria for receiving a fifteen-year renewal. Although the district review committee only recommended a five-year renewal, Superintendent Jackie Pons came through for us and recommended that the school board grant us a fifteen-year charter renewal, which they did. We were ecstatic!

Receiving a fifteen-year renewal was a wonderful ending to my years as the principal of the School of Arts and Sciences. I ended the 2011 school year satisfied with what we had accomplished and completely optimistic about the future of the school.

Chapter 5: Planning for Change

In the transition years when running the school made me the target of discontent; I thought that I might retire once I reached 30 years of service to education. However, when that time drew near, I decided to continue. It was important for me to leave the school in the best shape possible and we were facing big budget cuts as the state legislature began slicing funding for education. In addition, my cabin in Montana was not yet finished and I was in a relationship with a man whom I loved deeply. I was entertaining the notion of spending my life with him, so it made sense in every way to stay on course.

I kept planning for retirement by training someone on my staff whom I thought could take my place. I continued to live frugally and work on my Montana cabin in the summer financed by money that I saved during the school year. My Montana time became more and more precious to me and I went every summer to relax, enjoy the wilderness, and let all the school problems and worries slide off of me. In addition, I was in love and spent every weekend during the school year on my boyfriend's farm in South Georgia.

Then, early in the tenth year of the school, things changed radically for me. The man whom I thought of as the love of my life broke up with me, and I struggled through that year at school masking my grief and focusing on work. It is difficult to write about the despair that descended upon me and I longed to leave my life in Tallahassee behind and move to Montana. Although I wanted to run away, my commitment to the school kept me in place. Lucky for me, a co-counselor in North Carolina organized a support team of educational change leaders and one of the team called me every day at school to check in with me and give me a few minutes of one-way counseling time. This support helped me to continue on. I didn't talk much about my grief to people at work, but rather buried myself in the job.

One thing became clear to me. If I planned to leave the school, I needed to re-organize the administration. For this, I enlisted the thinking of two people who had been instrumental in the school's development. A consultant who works with small businesses was recommended to me, and I met with him over lunch to discuss the situation. With his advice in my mind, I planned for a re-organization. My biggest failing as a principal was not taking action on this sooner, but the situation was complicated by the prolonged illness of our assistant principal and my own personal struggles with a broken heart. I waited almost a year before I took action. By the time our school began its eleventh year, I knew that the time had come. The assistant principal was so ill by then that many tasks were not getting done and the workload of everyone in the office, including me, was unbearable.

In October, I discussed my administrative reorganization plan with all the key players and presented it to the board. Up to that point, the assistant principal was both the financial officer and the director of operations for the school. My plan involved separating the financial responsibilities out of the assistant principal's job description which would leave time for curriculum coordination. Best of all, the reorganization would occur with no increase in the school budget. On the day the board reviewed and approved the reorganization plan, our assistant principal took medical leave. Because we were fairly sure that she would not be returning to school, I moved to hire a new assistant principal and a financial services manager. A difficult two months followed as we figured out all of the tasks that had to be performed, but the result was an improvement in the administrative operations. I knew that I could not retire at the end of that year, however, because I needed to give the reorganization time to settle in.

The person I hired as the new assistant principal, Julie Fredrickson, was the person that I thought would make the best principal after I retired. She had been with the school since the beginning and was one of those teachers who were hired the year that the school did not open and ended up unemployed and scrambling for a job. She persevered that year and kept meeting to plan for the school's opening the following year. Once the school opened, the teachers saw her as a mentor and an advocate for them. She was already a major school leader, having served as the school advisory council chair and team leader throughout the history of the school.

Our twelfth year began better than ever. Our new assistant principal was working with teachers on curriculum and assessment and teachers felt that they were being supported wholeheartedly. Her love for teaching and teachers was evident to everyone around her. Although she had been an outstanding fourth/fifth grade classroom teacher who one would think would never leave the classroom, Julie took on her new job with enthusiasm and energy. Her superb organizational skills helped tremendously as she learned all of her new roles. For me, it was actually the first time that I had a real partner in leadership. Julie was someone who I could trust in every way. I trusted her thinking on issues even if they were different from mine. I trusted that she would back me and support me. Knowing that someone was standing under that burden of leadership with me was a great relief. I knew that she had my back and would always put the needs of the school first.

As a Montana friend told me, "Why not retire at the top of your game?" As I assessed the situation at school, I was pleased with how far we had come and how smoothly everything was running. I went back and forth in my mind that year many times—stay or go? It seemed like the right time to go.

On a personal level, I had spent that summer in Montana building a greenhouse/garage that would grow vegetables during the warm months and house my pickup truck during the cold months. My Montana cabin had been paid for as I built on it during the previous twelve summers and my Florida home would be paid off in a few months. I would be debt-free. I was ready to be free in every other way too. Thanks to the Florida Retirement System, with 34 years of service, I would have a pension that I thought I could live on. It was time.

I thought about all of the things I would have to give up: seeing students perform at Friday Sing each week, working with my team of creative, innovative teachers, my office that looked out on the garden, my spot on the Charter School Appeals Commission. I knew that I would spend the last semester with perpetual tears of goodbye in my eyes, but I was ready.

Iris Palazesi, the board chair, and I worked on a search plan to present to the board at the December meeting in 2010. The day before the meeting, I met with the office staff and the teachers to tell them that I was leaving at the end of the school year. I cried when I talked about the school and what it meant to me. That night, I called all of the board members individually to tell them. I submitted my written resignation at the board meeting the following night. A letter to the parents went home the next morning. On Friday, I spoke to the students about how people continue to learn and grow and take new steps in their lives. I explained to them that my new step would be to share what we had learned at the School of

Arts and Sciences with the rest of the world through writing a book and leading workshops to inspire other people to start schools like ours. Several students cried in my arms following Friday Sing (our weekly assembly program).

It was a busy and emotional week, but by the weekend, I felt renewed, free, and ecstatic about my decision. I had a new clarity about the next step in my life. I realized that my purpose was not just to establish this wonderful school for several hundred students but also to effect educational change on a wider playing field. Once the decision to retire was made, all kinds of new paths and possibilities opened before me. I knew that my winters and springs in Florida would be spent consulting and helping other innovative schools. There was talk of a new foundation to share the ideas that we had developed. I could see myself leading this endeavor. Someone suggested that we should start another kindergarten through eighth grade school on the other side of town based on our charter under the same board of directors. I could see myself helping to organize this new charter school. Suddenly, I could see many new roles for myself and I knew that my decision was a good one. In retrospect, I believe that I am a person that does not usually step into a vacuum. I have to see a new path filled with possibilities before I make my move. Despite all of the possibilities, my life went in entirely different directions once I was retired and had the freedom to dream new dreams.

From the moment that I announced my decision, the teachers took a major role in the process of finding a new principal. Their first step was to write a petition supporting Julie Fredrickson, the assistant principal, for the position. Twenty-four teachers signed the petition that was read by a teacher at a second board meeting in December. The teachers believed that it would be best if the new principal came from within the school in order to maintain the integrity of our mission and educational philosophy. They did not want to risk losing everything for which they had worked. I agreed with them, but understood why the board needed to have an open process.

The personnel committee met before the winter break to: revise the principal's job description, finalize a search plan, and write a job advertisement. After the break, the board met to officially approve the work of the committee. And so began a two and a half month process to find a new principal. This was a time of tension for the teachers and staff due to the unknown of who their next leader would be. This was a time of worry for me because, although I trusted the process, I was concerned about who my successor would be.

It was important to the board that the process for hiring the new principal be as transparent as possible and involve input from all of the school's stakeholders—students, parents, teachers, staff, and board. The position was advertised locally for three weeks as well as statewide and nationally. Applications were reviewed, telephone interviews were conducted, and in the end two applicants were invited to campus. Each of these candidates participated in five hours of interviews—first by the Search Committee, then selected student leaders, followed by teachers and staff, then the board, and finally parents. Each person who participated in the interviews was encouraged to fill out a comment card. The comments were compiled and given to the board to review before their vote was taken at the March board meeting. The outstanding part of this process took into account everyone's thinking—almost everyone's. The difficult part of this process for me was that I was not given a way to participate, except to introduce the candidates to each group who interviewed. Some thought that I would have too much influence over the process if I participated. However, due to my exclusion, I believe that the school was not given the chance to take advantage of my knowledge and expertise in what the job entails. Luckily, a former board chair spoke to the board about this disadvantage a few minutes before the final vote and a current board member stated that she wanted to hear my thinking. Not until that moment did I know that I would have the opportunity to share my insights. Even though it came late in the process, I was grateful for the opportunity.

After much discussion, the board voted to hire Julie Fredrickson as the new principal. The relief among the staff was almost palpable. I must admit that I relaxed for the first time in months. Throughout the hiring process, the board chair had told me that it was not too late to change my mind and stay, but I knew that the time was right. After Julie was chosen, I could finally admit to myself that I was leaving and passing the school on to another leader—one whom I trusted to do a good job.

The remaining months of school were filled with conducting annual evaluations, reappointing teachers to positions for the following year, organizing files, and training Julie. Sometimes I felt ecstatic about my pending retirement, and at other times I felt sad as the calendar marched toward the end of the school year. As the result of another large budget cut by the Florida Legislature, there were hard decisions to be made regarding teaching jobs and placements and budgets. I decided, and Julie eagerly agreed, that I would take responsibility for all of the hard decisions at the end of the year and take all the blame for those decisions so that she could begin her role as principal on the strongest and most positive note.

Over the years, I had learned that a leader has to make hard decisions based on what is best for the whole school and deal with the inevitable criticism. These decisions cannot be based on wanting to be liked but on wanting what is best. I was willing to do that one more time and spare the new principal.

The end of the school year came fast and furious. Toward the end, the students and teachers honored me at Friday Sing. I was dressed in a cape of paper hands made by the students and wore a crown as their queen. There were performances and videos recounting the history of the school and the part I had played. But the biggest surprise came after

Friday Sing. When I walked out of the auditorium after dismissing each class, I noticed that the whole school was gathered down by the new building. As I walked that way, I noticed the new lettering on the building that read: "Debo Powers Building." What a wonderful thing to realize that when I was no longer the principal, I would still be there, named on the side of the new building. I received hundreds of hugs that day and cried more than a few tears.

I looked back over the last thirteen years when my life and identity were defined by the school and wondered who I would be without it. I remembered the first few years when I could not introduce myself as the principal of the School of Arts and Sciences without giggling because my excitement was so great. I had evolved into a confident and competent leader over the years. Those thirteen years represented the greatest adventure of my life and one that had changed me for the better.

The evening after the last day of school, the board gave me a retirement party with dinner, an open bar, and dancing music. There were speeches by the new principal Julie Fredrickson, the board chair Iris Palazesi, and my dear friend and former principal of SAIL High School Rosanne Wood. I did a dance exhibition with John Burns, my dance competition partner, and then the floor was opened for dancing. It was a wonderful celebration of the school and my leadership.

I look back wistfully at those last days while staring at the mountains of Glacier National Park out of my cabin windows and feel satisfied with the work that I did and the things I accomplished. The school continues to thrive and innovate. It has moved on without me, just like it is supposed to do.

Section II: The Structure

Chapter 6: Just a Little Respect

I have a dream that my four little children will one day live in a nation where they will not be judged by the color of their skin but by the content of their character. I have a dream today. I have a dream that…little black boys and black girls will be able to join hands with little white boys and white girls as sisters and brothers. I have a dream today. --Dr. Martin Luther King, Jr. August 28, 1963

Developing and maintaining a climate of respect on campus is the foundation of our school. Our first task was to attract a diverse population of students. How to have a racially, culturally, and socioeconomically diverse school population was important in laying the groundwork for our commitment to creating a climate of respect on our campus. The question that we grappled with was: *How can we teach children how to live peacefully and respectfully in a multicultural world unless our school reflected the many cultures of the outside world?*

Once we had a diverse population of students at our school, the next task was to develop the school culture. Our philosophy on respect is not much different from what all good educators know. Susan Kovalik, the author of *ITI: The Model, Integrated Thematic Instruction* (Susan Kovalik & Associates, 1993), sums it up nicely by saying that the brain functions best in an environment where there is an absence of threat. People learn and function best when they know that they are loved and respected; where they are listened to and valued. It follows that the basis of any good school must be a climate of respect. This climate of respect is not something that can be achieved once and forgotten about. It must be nurtured constantly and valued above all else. Creating a respectful environment is a journey, a way of life, not an end product.

We started the development of a peaceful, respectful campus with ourselves, the teachers and staff. We made an annual commitment to treat each other with respect and talk directly when there was a difficulty rather than criticizing or gossiping behind each other's backs. We knew that our relationships were important and we made a pledge at the beginning of each year to honor those relationships. I attribute our school's climate of respect to the courage and commitment of the teachers in the relationships that they have developed with each other. As I said on the first pre-planning day: "This project rides on the quality of the relationships that we have with each other."

Listening exchanges have worked very well to provide a structure for school personnel to communicate with each other when issues threaten to divide us. This process provides a way for the participants to listen, show their feelings about how something has hurt them, and reach for solutions that will strengthen the relationship. It takes courage on both sides for a listening exchange to work well. The person requesting the listening exchange has to be brave enough to speak directly and the listener has to set aside his or her defensiveness to be able to listen well. With practice, we got better and better at using this process to work through relationship difficulties.

Dr. Becky Bailey's book *Conscious Discipline* (Loving Guidance, 2000) has had a major effect on our school community. We purchased a copy for each teacher and used it as a school-wide book study. Training was provided for teachers and parents at the school and a handful of teachers received week-long training at Dr. Bailey's seminars during summers. Dr. Bailey's statement that "No one can make you angry without your permission," from her first chapter on composure is particularly important for effective teaching and parenting. This chapter encourages people to be in charge of their own minds and not act on feelings of distress. Leaving our feelings of distress at the door when we enter a classroom has a magnificent effect on the entire school day. I might add that time needs to be set up outside the classroom for teachers to work on the feelings of distress that accumulate during the day.

In order to create a relaxed and less formal learning environment than in most schools, most of the teachers and staff were called by their first names rather than their last names by the students and parents. The same was true for me. Rather than referring to me as Ms. Powers, I was called Ms. Debo. This seemingly small change had enormous ramifications. It showed respect for our roles while communicating that we were accessible to all members of the school family.

Teachers did a considerable amount of work in the design of their classroom management practices to create an environment of respect. In setting up classroom rules, teachers opted for student-generated rules rather than teacher-imposed rules. This had the benefit of empowering students to help create a productive classroom. In our experience, students will propose rules that are similar to what the teacher would impose, but they are more likely to respect those rules because they had a voice in establishing them. Many times the students themselves will intervene with a student who is having difficulty and will help find solutions to a problem. For example, a student who is constantly disrupting the concentration of other students might be given the chance to hear from those students who will in turn listen to the offending student about what is going on for him or her. Misbehavior can often be corrected through caring and respectful communication among peers.

Teachers employed many different strategies for redirecting student misbehaviors. One of our teachers, Carly Beamish, is known for her "walk-abouts." When a student is having difficulty in class, she will sometimes take him or her on a walk around campus. This change of scenery, along with a little exercise and respectful conversation, can often shift the behavior of the student. This strategy is possible at our school because we have two teachers in the elementary classrooms.

Developing a culture of respect was hardest in the middle school. Because we started off with students in kindergarten through eighth grade, we had a few difficult years with the middle school. Our new middle school students had mostly come from large public middle schools where "put-downs" and disrespect were abundant. Now we were asking them to act in a different way and they had no model for this. In retrospect, the easier route would have been to start with the elementary grades and build the middle school over a few years with students who had internalized our philosophy in the younger grades. In subsequent years, this paid off. The elementary culture was carried into middle school with the students and we ended up having one of the safest and sweetest middle school environments imaginable.

However, things did not start off that smoothly. On the first day of school, the middle school teachers gathered the entire group together to share information and procedures with them. Having taught middle school students, I immediately recognized the barely contained mischievous tension among the students at that first meeting. Although there was the outward appearance of decorum, I sensed that they were biding their time until the meeting was over and they could run free like a bunch of wild colts getting into every kind of trouble they could think of. They seemed compelled to try to get away with everything that they possibly could. I caught one teacher's eye and we exchanged a nonverbal "uh oh." On that first day of school, I knew that it was going to take some time before we were able to convey to the students the picture of the kind of respectful and productive environment that we envisioned for our middle school.

Middle school is a tough time for young people. They are making the transition from childhood to the teen years and this transition creates a certain amount of anxiety and self-consciousness that often translates into acting out those insecurities at their peers. From the first day, we started working hard to create a respectful middle school.

My daughter was starting the eighth grade the first year that our school opened and she agreed to try out our school for a few days. I was hopeful that she would be a student there even though she had only one year left before going to high school. However, she immediately decided that she wanted to continue attending Full Flower School where she had been a student since kindergarten and where she had developed many close relationships. Although I was disappointed, I told her that the school was my project and it didn't have to be hers. She returned to Full Flower after just one day at our school.

I must say that I did not blame her. I knew that it was going to take months, possibly years to develop the middle school that we envisioned. Along the way to achieving an excellent middle school, there were elementary teachers frustrated by middle school behaviors who said, "Let's just get rid of the middle school and make this an elementary school." Luckily, we did not follow that path because the middle school that we ultimately developed over time is exemplary in both academic achievement and respectful culture.

As far as teaching the students about respect, we used everything that made sense to us—Peer Mediation, Peace Works, Path of the Peaceful Warrior, Life Skills, Co-counseling, and Conscious Discipline. We used a variety of programs, but what we learned is that having a respectful school requires constant vigilance and using the teachable moments as they occur. Once we had a full-time guidance counselor on staff, she developed a program to prevent bullying and disrespect among the students. Her curriculum provides a weekly guidance lesson with hands-on activities in every classroom. In addition, there is a three-day seminar for middle school students at the end of the first semester. The focus of the guidance curriculum has always been on teaching listening skills and peaceful conflict resolution.

Before we had a guidance counselor on campus, I served as the school's number one listener. Teachers regularly sent me students who were too upset to be in the classroom. I spent hours listening to young people each week. Sometimes they just needed to talk to someone. Other times they expressed feelings through tears, laughter, shaking, or raging. I recognized these things as symptoms of emotional healing. I gave these students my attention and caring until they calmed down and were ready to go back to class. Too many times adults interrupt the natural healing process and leave young people with unresolved hurts. I just listened respectfully to them and pointed them in a positive direction if they were overwhelmed by counterproductive feelings. Being treated with respect by the principal is very validating to young people who often feel powerless and insignificant in our society.

Harvey Jackins in *The Human Side of Human Beings* (Rational Island Publishers, 1972) says that human beings have an inherent nature that is good, loving, cooperative, intelligent, zestful about life, and connected to all living things. Any exhibited attitude or behavior that is contrary to this picture is the result of the person having been hurt and acting on the basis of that hurt rather than his/her clear, intelligent thinking. When a person gets hurts, a distress recording is installed that clouds the thinking and produces negative or ineffective ways of functioning. These hurts can be healed. According to Jackins, when free of distress humans have a vast intelligence that is capable of developing unique solutions to all of the problems facing humanity.

This theory makes sense to me when thinking about students and what gets in the way of their ability to learn and function cooperatively. A student who has received the message that he is stupid will not function well in school. A young person who has received messages from the society that she is a second class citizen for whatever reason (gender, race, ethnicity, class), will not be free to learn and develop to her highest potential. Good schools are those where these negative messages are contradicted and where each student is treated with complete respect at all times.

In addition to our other programs to build respect, our students are involved in empathy training to help them understand and respect students with disabilities. Volunteers from CARD (Center for Autism and Related Disabilities) come to our school to lead workshops for the classrooms where there are students with Asperger Syndrome or similar disabilities. We have found that when students understand the reason why some students are behaving differently, they are very empathetic and respectful to that student and his/her differences.

The student council did a lot of work to engender respect on campus. There were even two unique positions on the council called "secretary of peace" and "secretary of diversity." These positions were filled by the same school-wide election process that was used for electing the student council president and vice president. It was the job of the secretary of peace to give out Peacemaker Awards during each Friday Sing. Students were chosen for these awards by their teachers for demonstrating life skills, such as respect, collaboration, and trustworthiness. The secretary of diversity worked with the secretary of peace on issues of respect. For many years during the beginning of our school, the students holding these two positions organized a "day of respect" that included activities, discussions, and performances.

Another way that we worked with students was to teach them how to interrupt (stand up against) oppressive attitudes when they witnessed them. When people hear oppressive things, they tend to freeze and be silent in order to avoid becoming the target. Encouraging young people to speak up rather than to go silent, empowers them to trust their own thinking and take responsibility for creating a world based on respect for others.

Even after our culture of respect was firmly in place, we noticed that from time to time a new student would come to our school full of fight and attitude. We gave those students extra positive attention because it was clear that they carried a great deal of hurt from a less respectful school culture. In most cases, we were able to show these students that they were safe here; that they could relax and be kids and not have to be ready to defend themselves all of the time. Watching this transition was very gratifying for the entire staff although it took a great deal of patience and persistence to get there.

Our suspension rate was very low. There was not a single year when the number of students who got into fights was more than could be counted on one hand. Some years, the number was zero. These so-called fights were usually no more than shoving matches caused by short tempers on the playground, but this was handled by a process with the students talking out the problem in my office and going home for the rest of the day. (Going home for the rest of the school day was what we called suspension.) Because our students liked being with their peers while being engaged in hands-on learning, they did not want to be sent away for the day.

I believe that if you want a young person to respect you, you have to first treat him or her with respect. As the principal, I made a point of treating all misbehaving students with complete respect while calmly following through with the agreed upon consequences for the misbehavior. Showing the student respect included listening to him or her and trying to figure out what was at the root of the misbehavior so that the student could get some help with what caused the difficulty.

Having a small school (under 300 students) helps in building a respectful environment by the simple fact that everyone knows everyone else. Dehumanizing others is more difficult in a small community where you know everyone and their families. Our school is like a big family.

One day during Friday Sing, a girl walked forward on the stage toward the microphone and she stumbled and caught herself. She looked at the audience with the kind of fear in her eyes of someone who knows that she will be teased and ridiculed. In most school settings, there would have been laughter causing her embarrassment that might have robbed her of a confident performance. Just a little stumble and everything could change. I held my breath. *Not one person laughed.* She looked surprised, but walked confidently to the microphone and continued. I was exhilarated because this was clear evidence that what we were doing was working!

Every day on campus, one can see the kind of world that we are creating. One of the greatest joys for me is watching the close friendships of the students from every racial, ethnic, religious, and socioeconomic background. I love watching little children from all backgrounds holding hands on the playground. It is truly the realization of Dr. King's dream of friendship and love among all people. I got to see that dream come true in my lifetime.

Chapter 7: Our Innovative Curriculum

Education is the most powerful weapon which
you can use to change the world.

Nelson Mandela

Creating an innovative school is not an easy task because there are few models. Following a traditional model is easier, but I believe that charter schools should be innovative. The opportunity to start a new school with public funding comes with a responsibility to create something different from the traditional public school model. Although many charter schools in our state are very similar to what is provided through the district school system, a truly great charter school will offer parents and students something different. The curriculum design of our school is indeed something distinctive from what is found in traditional public schools, even in a district as good as ours.

In order to avoid replicating the traditional "factory model" of education, we designed our classrooms differently with tables and groupings of students. As our school grew and we were able to acquire more, we filled the classrooms with research materials and computers that can be used by the students as they develop projects for their thematic units. They have access to supplies for making posters, dioramas, and PowerPoint presentations.

We believe that learning is a joyous process, that the human brain *wants* to learn and that we only need to set up the right conditions to give that natural process a chance to happen. The teachers at our school develop the curriculum in interdisciplinary thematic units that incorporate social studies, science, and literature and where students do copious amounts of reading and writing on the theme topics. The teaching methods include some lecture by the teacher, but mostly hands-on activities, student research, cooperative learning, project development, and presentations by students. Teachers serve as facilitators and organizers for the learning process. The students are actively engaged and the classrooms buzz like beehives.

Although we have enough classroom spaces to have a different room for each grade, another unique feature of our school is that classrooms are multi-age, meaning that more than one grade is taught in each classroom. There are four clusters: kindergarten and first grade classes, second and third grade classes, fourth and fifth grade classes at the elementary level and sixth, seventh, and eighth grades in the middle school classes.

There are several advantages to a multi-age classroom. First, students have the same teacher for more than one year. The relationship between the teacher and students and their families can be developed more fully over a two-year or three-year period. As a result, in the elementary classrooms only half of the students are new to the teacher each year. In the middle school classrooms, only one-third are new. Next, older students develop their leadership skills and self-esteem by helping younger students. And, younger students have older models to emulate. For example, the kindergarteners try to do the things that the first graders can already do. It is inspiring for them. In addition, it reinforces the learning of the first graders when they show a kindergartener how to do something. They feel so smart! According to Dr. Carolyn Schluck, multi-age classrooms result in "a gradual raising of the standards" as the younger students learn from the older students and begin to function on a higher level than they would in a one-grade classroom.

In the primary grades (kindergarten and first), the classrooms are full of hands-on equipment and materials. The children at this age are concrete learners rather than abstract learners and have the opportunity at our school to touch and manipulate objects that aids the learning process. Although we are not a strictly Montessori school, we use many of the Montessori materials because they are excellent resources for teaching skills in a concrete way. Kindergarten and first grade students use a variety of math manipulatives to learn place value, addition, multiplication, and subtraction. They use objects to practice sounds and letters and a movable alphabet to spell out words. Our primary teachers receive training in how to best use the materials and how to train the students to use them. A word of thanks goes to our first assistant principal, Jane Wofford, who brought Montessori methods to our school and trained teachers in the use of Montessori equipment. Visitors to our school find the primary classes especially interesting because they observe these very young children independently working with hands-on equipment at their individual level of ability. The students are often so focused on their tasks that they do not even notice the visitors in the classroom.

Emergent reading is given a great deal of attention in the primary classrooms, as well as writing and publishing. Students participate in the "A to Z" guided reading program in small groups based on their ability rather than their grade level. One primary teacher wrote and received a grant with which the kindergarten and first grade team purchased leveled books that the students can take home to read aloud to their parents. After reading the text three times at home, the students demonstrate to one of their teachers that they can read the text fluently after which they get another book to take home. For those students who do not have involved parents, the teachers find time to listen to those students read their book as part of their daily intervention strategy. Students also work on language and reading skills through Montessori materials, teacher-generated games and activities, small group lessons, and conferencing individually with teachers. As the students progress to the higher elementary levels, they become much more independent as learners and their reading becomes much more content based. As the common core standards have moved into the state educational system in the past few years, teachers at our school have realized that they have been doing the right things for their students all along.

Primary students write and illustrate in their journals every day. Sometimes the teachers assign a topic and sometimes it is "writer's choice." Teachers conference with students every day on their writing and help them edit their work. When a student is ready to publish something that is important to them, they type, format, print, illustrate, and bind their story into a small book. The student can then sign up to read their story to the class in the "author's chair." The student decides whether to take their book home or put it in their portfolio. As the students progress and begin reading chapter books, they are motivated to write chapter books and their published works get longer and more sophisticated. Writing is infused into the thematic curriculum to a greater and greater extent as students move into higher grade levels.

Besides the basic skills taught in the primary grades, students begin at this early age to develop their independence as learners. This is an important skill in a school with a curriculum like ours and developmentally-appropriate methods are used at every grade level cluster to foster the skills needed for students to take charge of their learning. For instance, in a kindergarten and first grade classroom, a student learns how to independently take the materials for a lesson off the shelf, complete the work, and return the materials to the shelf in an organized way so that they are ready for the next student to use. These early skills set the stage for more and more independence. By second and third grade, students are developing projects at the end of each thematic unit. Classroom "showcases" provide a time for students to display their project and talk about what they learned. Parents and the students from other classes visit the classroom to see the projects. By the time a student is in a fourth and fifth grade classroom, the projects and showcases become more sophisticated and they are researching independently and making PowerPoint presentations to the class.

Two teachers are assigned to every elementary classroom—a lead teacher and an associate teacher. Although they work as a team, the two teachers are paid differently and have different responsibilities. The lead teacher is ultimately held responsible for the curriculum, assessment, and progress of the students. The associate teacher works with the lead teacher as a united team throughout the day, but is free on nights and weekends from the task of curriculum development outside of school time. We often hire young people right out of college with teaching certificates but no teaching experience in the job of associate teacher. As they gain expertise, they are eligible to become lead teachers when there are openings. In this way, we have our own teacher training program to prepare teachers for the rigors of being a lead teacher (and curriculum developer) in a school like ours.

There are many other advantages to having two teachers in the classroom. For one, managing a hands-on classroom is much more effective with two teachers because they can both circulate throughout the classroom to help students who are working on projects. Two, the classroom can be divided into two separate groups for various activities or discussions. This allows for a tremendous amount of flexibility in the classroom. Groups can be arranged based on any number of reasons. Third, a big advantage is that when one teacher is absent, the other can facilitate the classroom activities for that day and no time is lost for the students, as often happens with substitute teachers. An added benefit is that the school generally does not have to hire a substitute to replace a teacher who has to miss school.

It is important to note that the associate teacher position evolved between the time of the original charter design to the reality of managing the school. The founders envisioned associate teachers who would move more flexibly from classroom to classroom bringing their talents and skills to different classrooms. However, from the beginning we saw the value of having two teachers in each classroom to facilitate the hands-on curriculum. The assignment of an associate to every elementary classroom was instrumental in the success of our program. The idea of associate teachers was adopted by our district school system on a limited basis in later years to solve some of their class size issues. This is an example of an innovative idea from a charter school being used by the district system.

Every semester, we have a large group of practicum students from Florida State University. In later years, we added students from Thomas University. These practicum students offer a great deal to the classrooms in which they work. Having extra adults in classrooms where students are engaged in independent learning and project development is always helpful. These college students get to participate in an innovative program that differs from the traditional settings where they have been receiving their education. This is a good way for us to disseminate our educational philosophy and ideas to prospective teachers who will most likely be working in traditional schools.

With the multi-age classrooms, teachers must develop themes in a two-year wheel for elementary and three-year wheel for middle school. Themes unify information from many disciplines, such as history, science, language arts, geography, and art. An example of a theme might be "oceans" and this thematic study could involve projects related to marine biology, geography of oceans, political ramifications of oil spills, chemical analysis of seawater, stories and poems about the ocean. Admittedly, in the early years of our school, teachers chose themes from ideas that interested them. However, as accountability in the form of standardized tests became the norm for all public schools, teachers had to develop their themes based on state standards for the grades covered. There have been times where the state standards have changed and teachers have had to discard beautiful thematic units that they have developed and start all over again.

Elementary teachers meet to determine the themes that will be taught in a two-year wheel that covers the state standards for the grade levels in their classrooms. Within each cluster, they divvy up the tasks of developing the activities and lessons for each thematic unit. If the unit was previously developed in another school year, they evaluate what was successful and revise the unit to better meet the needs of the students. In this way, the thematic units improve over time.

Thematic project-based learning is a key part of our curriculum. Students develop projects based on the themes that they are studying. These projects are displayed for others to view. In addition, students make presentations to share what they have learned with classmates. Following their presentations, students field questions from their audience. Over the years, our students become adept at making presentations and feeling comfortable in front of a group. Hallie Gaudio, a former student, told me that when she went to high school, she was amazed by how uncomfortable other students were when asked to make a class presentation. She had grown up thinking that was the norm. Our students tend to excel in other educational settings and the job market because of their presentation skills.

In our middle school, students change classes every period and have lockers for their books and materials. Every student takes math, language arts, social studies, and science and these core subjects are taught by highly qualified teachers in those fields. In these ways, we resemble traditional middle schools. However, students are in multi-age classrooms with sixth, seventh, and eighth graders. Each teacher develops a three-year wheel of themes that cover the state standards for their subject area. In the course of three years, a student will cover all of the areas that the state deems necessary for their middle school years, but they will address this material in a different sequence and using very different methods than in most schools. For instance, students can show that they have mastered standards in many creative ways rather than just take a test. They often develop comprehensive projects that are judged by a rubric. They also attack the academic content in each core course in a variety of creative ways, such as hands-on science experiments, social studies simulations, speaker's forums, and math contests. We have one lead teacher for each core subject area and one associate teacher who is shared among the lead teachers.

The teaching methods used by our middle school team are exemplary and have resulted in student FCAT scores that surpass the district and state averages. We have constantly worried that the trend toward statewide standardized "end-of-course exams" will destroy the three-year curriculum wheels in our middle school classrooms. It will be interesting to see how the school deals with this challenge to our very successful curriculum structure.

In many middle schools, language arts, math, and science get most of the attention and resources because those are the content areas that are found on the statewide standardized assessment. Social studies is considered less important. Because I was a secondary social studies teacher before becoming a principal, I understood the importance of studying history, government, economics, and civics in order to be an informed citizen in a democratic society. Luckily, I found just the right teacher to bring these things alive for our middle school students. Whereas social studies in many traditional schools can be as dry as dust, the students in Michelle Zieman's classes grapple with the topics and issues in a way that they will never forget. Throughout their three years in middle school, they participate in simulated historical events, such as the US Constitutional Convention in 1787 or a sweat shop during the Industrial Revolution. They sit on panels as experts on rainforests taking the (assigned) perspective of a logger, a politician, or an environmental activist. Michelle is always careful to expose students to a vast array of opinions so that they have to think, question, research, evaluate, and reach their own conclusions. The thinking, writing, and presenting that the students do in social studies carries over into all other areas of learning.

Each year, every middle school student participates in the history fair. In groups or as individuals, they create history projects that are judged by a panel of professionals outside of the school community. The thinking and sophistication of many of these projects is astounding. The skills learned have given our students a significant advantage in high school and college.

Basing our themes on the content required by the state standards is about as far as we go toward "teaching to the test." From the start of our school, the teachers were adamant that we would "not let the FCAT drive our boat!" Teachers had witnessed how so much attention on the outcome of a standardized test can squeeze all of the creativity and excitement out of learning, as well as teaching, and they wanted no part in it. They refused to participate in the practice of "drill and kill" where the students are drilled on material every day, thus killing the joy of learning. Our theory is based on the notion that if students are excited about learning and are reading and writing in thematic units which cover state standards, they will be successful on the state test. This has proven to be the case. Since 2003 when the State of Florida began to count our scores toward a school grade, our test scores have given our school an "A" grade every year.

As you can imagine, thematic curriculum development takes an enormous amount of work. Some teachers have the creativity, passion, and commitment to pursue this style of teaching regardless of the amount of time that it takes. Other teachers have decided after teaching at our school that our curriculum expectations are too high and have left our school to return to traditional public schools with textbooks and "boxed" curriculum. The teachers who have stayed year after year are the true heroes of our school. Without them, we would never have been successful with this curriculum model. They have sacrificed free time and family time to think, plan, and produce dynamic lessons and activities for their students. They have made a difference in the world—in the lives of their students, the reputation of the school, and the cause of educational change. They have shown that students can be successful learners while having fun and being creative at the same time.

After hearing about our curriculum design, many educators have commented that our program is similar to a gifted program in philosophy. If that comparison can be made, then it is "gifted education for everyone." All of our students are given the opportunity to explore and "think outside the box." In addition, all of our classrooms are inclusion classrooms because our student population has all levels of ability. While some people think that charter schools take all of the most advanced students, that is not the case with a lottery system. Our student population has about 20-25 percent with learning disabilities and about 5-10 percent gifted. The other students fall everywhere in between. Effort is made to meet the needs of all of these different ability levels through our thematic, project-based curriculum.

Our special education program is an inclusion program. Students with learning disabilities are placed in regular academic classrooms. Special education teachers come into the regular classrooms to work with students with learning disabilities in areas where they need extra instruction and help. Sometimes students with disabilities have a federally-funded aide who works one-on-one with them throughout the day during their regular classroom experiences. At times, a small group of students may be pulled out of their regular classroom to receive special instruction. In addition to the special education program, interventions are provided to students achieving below grade level and extensions are provided for those students who need the challenge of going further, faster, or deeper. Students whose disabilities are too severe for them to function in a regular classroom are provided services at special programs within the district.

Over the years, we learned how to use student performance data to help in planning curriculum and interventions for struggling students. In the early years, the teachers and I were resistant to the use of data from standardized testing. We feared that it might force us to squeeze out the innovation inherent in our curriculum design. However, over the years we learned how to use data to make our academic program more successful for specific learners. One teacher, Eirin Lombardo, was particularly good at making sense out of data and she headed up our data team. Under her leadership, teachers learned to use data to improve their instruction. Assistant Principal Julie Fredrickson also helped introduce teachers to new methods for gathering on-going data about their students' progress. As a group of educators, we have continued to grow and expand our knowledge about ways to help our students rather than rigidly sticking to old ideas.

One unique component of our school is the student portfolio. Students update their portfolio with their best work at the end of each semester. At the elementary level, portfolios are organized using Howard Gardner's Eight Intelligences. Projects and work are categorized under one of the intelligences, such as linguistic, spatial, kinesthetic, musical, mathematical, and interpersonal. While most schools only focus on linguistic and mathematical intelligence, we recognize and celebrate the fact that there are many different types of intelligence. The progression of a student's portfolio from kindergarten to eighth grade demonstrates the growth in the student's ability to think critically and analyze situations.

Middle school students write reflections for their portfolios on the projects and activities that meant the most to them in terms of their learning. Although the middle school portfolio is organized by subject area rather than by the eight intelligences, one part of their reflection relates to the types of intelligence that were demonstrated in a specific project. A middle school student's portfolio usually occupies a huge binder filled with an impressive amount of thinking and reflection. These portfolios are treasured by many students long after they have graduated and gone on to high school and college.

We use "early release days" at the end of each semester for parents and students to meet individually with teachers to go over the portfolio and discuss the student's progress. This gives parents more information than a grade on a report card. Standard grades are not given at our school; rather a progress report communicates a student's growth. Portfolios are an integral part of the curriculum and assessment of students.

One thing that we learned over time is that math cannot be covered sufficiently in our interdisciplinary thematic units. We add math into themes whenever possible, but the learning of math is rigorous, sequential, and requires systematic and daily exposure in order to adequately cover the state standards and learn the necessary skills. This is one place in our curriculum where we have had to adjust our practice in order to meet the needs of our students. While our reading scores were much higher than the district and state averages (89-90 percent proficiency), our elementary math scores were a bit lower. This made us reevaluate the way that math was being taught. We decided to buy a math program. The teachers piloted lessons from different math programs and voted unanimously on the one that was the most consistent with our teaching methods and educational philosophy. Because we are a charter school, we had the freedom to choose what works best for us rather than what the district uses. As the result of using a systematic program that correlates to the state standards, students gain essential math skills and our math scores have markedly increased to surpass district and state averages at every grade level.

As befits our school name, we have an exemplary program of arts and sciences. Science receives extra attention in the younger grades. From kindergarten on, students have the opportunity to be scientists: to question and inquire, to make hypotheses and experiment, to observe and analyze. For the elementary grades, we have a dedicated science resource teacher who brings hands-on science lessons into each classroom whenever they are studying a science-related theme. In addition, all elementary students have a weekly gardening class. As these students plant, weed, harvest, and cook from the gardens, there are many hands-on opportunities to learn about soil, photosynthesis, bugs, and plant diseases. They gain a connection with the land and where their food comes from. Our belief is that young people who have the opportunity to interact with the natural world and notice their connection to it will be better able to think about and address the environmental issues facing the world. In addition, students learn to enjoy growing and eating various foods that they otherwise might not like. As a result of our gardening program, beautiful organic gardens adorn our campus producing flowers, herbs, and vegetables.

Our middle school science program offers more hands-on science than many college courses. I often brag that I stole our middle school science teacher from a district school. I had heard Julie Sear speak at a district meeting about how she taught science and afterwards I told her that she should come to work at our school where she would have the freedom and encouragement to continue to develop her hands-on science program. When we had an opening, I called her and asked if she wanted the job. After some negotiation, she accepted and this has been a major blessing for our school. Julie teaches science like it should be taught. The students are actively engaged in science. They run experiments, observe, record their data, and reach conclusions just like actual scientists in the field. They make models and explain scientific concepts. In addition, Julie is a master at using a "smart board" to bring the latest discoveries in science right into her classroom.

In addition, we have a science mentorship program for middle school students who are gifted or talented in science. In this program, they work in teams of two with scientists from the community in laboratories every Friday morning for three hours. Second semester for these students is always at the National High Magnetic Field Laboratory at Florida State University where ground-breaking science is taking place daily. At the end of each semester, mentorship students spend an evening giving PowerPoint presentations on the research they have conducted during that semester. Parents, teachers, and the scientists who have served as mentors attend these presentations. After being immersed in science since kindergarten, our scores on the state assessment for eighth grade science are some of the highest in the entire state.

From the very beginning of our school, we believed that everyone is an artist and needs the opportunity to develop their artistic talents. Despite budget cuts, we have held on to our arts program tenaciously. A variety of classes are offered in music, drama, art, dance, band, media productions, and photography. Many gifted artists have taught at our school. In addition, art is integrated into thematic units and can be seen throughout classrooms and student projects.

One way that we showcase our school's artistic talent is through our weekly Friday Sing program. Every Friday, the entire school goes to the auditorium for Friday Sing. Each classroom has the opportunity to host Friday Sing several times each year. In addition, students and teachers can sign up to perform at Friday Sing. The student hosts organize the program and announce each performance. Every week is different. Students and teachers sing, dance, act, play musical instruments, read poems, tell jokes, and demonstrate karate-- whatever. There are certain favorite songs that the whole school sings together. Students are recognized as "peacemakers" for exemplary behavior. Sometimes a class presents a theme performance to show what they have been learning. Sometimes the dance, band, or music class performs. Teachers are encouraged to perform also. We even have our own "Dancing with the Stars" when the principal does a ballroom or swing dance exhibition on stage with a dance pro. Parents often attend to watch their children perform onstage.

Besides showing off our talents, Friday Sing gives students the chance to practice their public speaking skills. At our school, we believe that this is an important skill for everyone to acquire and one that cannot be tested on a standardized assessment. Most adults list public speaking as the thing that scares them the most and I often wonder how much this fear has limited people's lives. I do not think that our students will carry this limitation with them throughout their lives because speaking in public is a normal and natural thing that everyone does at our school. The school's climate of respect makes this possible because there is very little chance that someone will be laughed at or ridiculed. Students as young as five are comfortable being on stage speaking into the microphone in front of a packed crowd. This kind of confidence and self-assurance will carry them a long way in life.

Friday Sing also gives us the chance to practice showing respect for each other and being a good audience every week. When our students attend a performance off-campus, people always comment about what a good audience they are. That is because they have had weekly practice. Friday Sing is an integral part of our curriculum. It is the heart and soul of our school. Everything comes together there—creativity, respect, fun, learning, appreciation, courage, and unity. Friday Sing is where we celebrate our school community every week.

The teaching of foreign languages is one area of the curriculum where we have continually struggled to meet our goals. Although we have found the resources to provide two teachers in the elementary classrooms and an exemplary program of arts and sciences, funding a meaningful foreign language program has been difficult. We have done our best over the years. Sometimes we have had a Spanish teacher on staff and at other times we have had graduate students from Florida State University's Modern Language Department who taught once a week in each elementary classroom. Students were exposed to Japanese, German, French, Spanish, and Russian. For a year or two, a parent volunteer taught Latin in the middle school. Residing in the state of Florida, focusing on the teaching of Spanish made the most sense to us due to the large numbers of Spanish-speakers in our state. Our dream would be to have a comprehensive program where students were fluent in Spanish before leaving the eighth grade. With budget cuts, we have not yet been able to reach this goal.

Most people would not include a description of the extended day program in a discussion about the school's curriculum. However, at the School of Arts and Sciences, the extended day program (EDP) is actually an extension of the school's educational program. The same climate of respect characterizes EDP as during the school day. There is a strong emphasis on the arts and hands-on learning. Students can sign up for classes and workshops that interest them. These include everything from cooking to designing scrapbooks to playing a musical instrument. A string band practices weekly and performs at the Florida Folk Festival each year. Kate Taluga designed the program in our school's first year of operation and remains the program's director to this day. Students love being a part of this innovative program.

The culmination of every school year is the eighth grade graduation celebration. Our graduation celebration is fairly unique, although we copied the graduation format from SAIL High School where I had previously taught. What makes our graduation exciting is that a teacher goes on stage with each graduate and shares with the audience the graduate's strengths and unique personality. The teachers' creative presentations have become an art form in itself as the audience gets a picture of each graduate in the form of beautiful tributes, tear-jerking descriptions of challenges and successes, and often humor. The event is truly the highlight of the school year and is a fitting way to send our students off to high school knowing that they are deeply valued as individuals.

We are justifiably proud of our innovative curriculum and enjoy showing it off. During each school year, we have many visitors to campus who wish to see our program in action. Every week, the principal leads a school tour that is open to anyone who wants to come. The tour includes a presentation on the educational philosophy of the school. Not only do prospective parents attend these tours before enrolling their students in the lottery, but many educators both locally and from other districts and states attend in order to gain new perspectives on education. Most of us started this school, not only to create a wonderful learning environment for a small group of young people, but to change education everywhere. Our weekly tour is one way that we spread our ideas and successes to people outside of our school.

Chapter 8: Financial Responsibility

Judicious financial management is absolutely necessary for a successful charter school. The principal of a charter school is not only the educational leader, but s/he is the CEO of the organization and must think like one. Because most charter school principals are hired for their educational experience rather than their financial experience, they need to surround themselves with people who have a background in finance. Many charter schools fail because they have not handled their money wisely. When a charter school is given permission to operate using public funds, the school has an obligation and responsibility to spend those public funds prudently. This responsibility amounts to a sacred trust.

From the very beginning, we took this responsibility seriously and made sure that everyone who was dealing with the school finances was well trained and honest. Throughout the history of the school, the three people who have served as the school's financial officer (John Smith, Jane Wofford, and Anthony Gaudio, consecutively) were fiscally conservative in their management of the school's budget. They were frugal and cut waste whenever it was discovered. There were checks and balances in our financial procedures and oversight by the board's finance committee. For example, although the principal and financial officer develop the budget, the finance committee reviews it and recommends changes before it goes to the board for a final vote. As we matured as a charter school, we attracted people with extensive financial experience to our board so that they could serve on the finance committee. This expertise has been invaluable.

While it is important to run a charter school like a business, the dilemma for charter schools lies in the fact that to create a world class educational program, you cannot run your charter school exclusively like a business. The education of students has to be the priority. This means having a first-rate teaching staff and that is not cheap. About 84 percent of our school budget goes to staff salaries and benefits.

In order to have the rich academic program that characterizes our school, we have put as many resources into the classroom as possible. In order to have two teachers in every elementary classroom and an extensive art and science program, we have had to develop a very lean budget. We have found many ways to save money while providing our lead teachers with comparable salaries and benefits to the teachers who work for the district. For example, when we created our first budget, it was suggested that we use a 401k plan for teacher retirement. I was adamant that in order to attract good teachers, we needed to be in the Florida Retirement System (FRS). Although FRS cost the school more than a 401k plan would have, it was a superior retirement program and contributed to our ability to attract good teachers.

There have been times that we have not been able to give the same level of raises to our lead teachers as the district because of budget constraints, but we have made every effort to catch up when we could. The place where we cannot financially come close to the district pay scale is in the salaries of veteran teachers. This is why many charter schools tend to hire younger teachers who are not so high on the pay scale. At our school, lead teachers have to decide for themselves whether or not to stay at our school once they have reached the upper levels of their profession because they can make more money with the district.

In addition to this, we decided to use the district's health insurance for our teachers. We are able to compensate teachers for a similar portion of individual health insurance as the district. An added benefit, not given by the district, is that we provide the same amount of compensation to teachers if they are covered by another health plan through their spouse. However, we cannot afford to compensate a family insurance plan at the same rate as the district. For this reason, some teachers who need compensation for a family plan have made the decision to return to the district.

While it is financially difficult to devote a large percentage of the revenues to the classroom and pay teachers near the going rate, it pays off in the results you get in the performance of the students and their ability to learn. While our charter school is a not-for-profit school, there are some for-profit management companies running charter schools. For-profit charter schools put a smaller percentage of their revenues into the classroom than we were able to do. They accomplish this by paying their teachers less than the going wage in the sponsoring district. In some cases they have decided to pay teachers the equivalent of beginning teacher salaries across the board whether they are first year teachers or experienced ones with advanced degrees. This model is good for the bottom line but does little to create the kind of charter school that excels in student progress.

We were able to overcome financial difficulty by judicious use of resources, lower than average facility costs, replacement of paid staff with volunteers in the early years, making do with less than perfect equipment, and supplementing state revenues with donations and grants. Another important component was creating a school community that was invested in the school's success. Parents contributed not only time but money to the school. For instance, one family made sure that the school received several grants from a family trust, the Rintels Foundation, for various programs at the school, including the elementary science resource program. In addition, many families signed up for regular bank drafts to keep the science program alive during the years of severe budget cuts by the state legislature. Others donated or raised money for the school in a variety of ways. Without the commitment of these parents and community members, we would not have been able to sustain the quality science program that we had. In addition, our parent organization raised money every year that went toward improvements on campus that we could not have afforded otherwise.

Along with allocating resources to support an exemplary academic program, a good charter school needs to plan for the future by putting some money into reserves each year. We were able to do this every year that I was the principal. Our reserves have given us the freedom to dream of bigger and better things, such as building a new building, improving technology, creating a media center, and planning for future school expansion.

The amount of money that comes to our school from the state has never been enough for what we wanted to accomplish, even before the massive budget cuts that have plagued education during the recession years. Despite a strong commitment to frugal financial management, one thing that hinders charter schools is the disparity between the tax payer dollars that go to charter schools as opposed to regular public schools. For example, although Leon County voters approved a half-penny sales tax for public schools in our district, charter schools have not been included in the allocation of those funds. While district schools spent this additional revenue on new buildings and technology, we had to find other sources to fund these things. For example, in order to purchase student computers, teacher laptops, and smart boards for the classrooms, we had to rely on grants. As the principal, I wrote three grants each totaling around $100,000 that helped us pay for technology. In addition, parent and board member Mark Baldino, who worked for IBM, obtained further grants from his company to help us with technology. However, these grants were a drop in the bucket compared to the amount of revenue we would have received from the half-penny sales tax. To build our new building, we had to refinance our property in order to free up construction money. In recent years, the board has begun having a major fundraiser each year to raise money for capital projects. Our burden would be greatly decreased if we were recipients of the half-penny sales tax like other public schools.

Capital funding for charter schools is also very difficult to manage. Each year, the Florida State Legislature allocates a pot of money for charter school capital funding. This pot of money is divvied up between all of the charter schools in the state based on student enrollment. The amount changes from month-to-month as the number of charter school students in the state rises. The amount of money allocated to the capital funding pot has not changed much in many years while the number of charter schools in the state continues to grow rapidly. As the number of charter schools increases, the allocation per student decreases. Unfortunately, this pits charter schools against each other in the scramble for funds. It is an extreme hardship on schools that signed mortgages for buildings and have fewer dollars to pay these bills each year.

This situation keeps the financial wizards at our school busy figuring out how to make ends meet.

During my time as principal, managing our small charter school in a fiscally responsible way became harder and harder due to cuts in the per-pupil allocation for public schools from the State of Florida. Larger schools can operate with more economies of scale and many of the state's charter school policies favor these larger schools. For this reason, we have tried to expand our student population over time to mitigate the effects of budget cuts without jeopardizing or decreasing our educational programs. We have explored ways to increase the size of our campus or purchase other property and move there.

Making the hard decisions regarding the school budget falls on the school principal who must make recommendations to the board. He or she is the person in the best position to know which programs must be cut and which ones need to be preserved. Because these decisions affect people's jobs and the programs available for children, these decisions can be fraught with emotion and pressure from all those affected. During the recession years when we had to figure out how to operate with a balanced budget despite lower state revenues, many hard decisions had to be made. We utilized public forums so that parents and staff could voice their opinions, but in the end the principal ultimately had to make the difficult decisions.

One area that causes funding difficulties in a small charter school like ours is the special education program.

Although our district has always been fair in making sure that we received the appropriate amount of funds designated for special education based on the number of students with disabilities that we serve (20-25 percent in our case), our inclusion program has always cost us more than our federal allocation for those services. Since our main goal is to meet the needs of all our students, we just accepted the fact that we would need to spend more resources in this area. As a result of this extra resource allocation, students with disabilities do very well at our school. However, in years with state-wide budget cuts, we could not augment our special education program as we would have liked. This was one program that had to be cut back somewhat which meant fewer hours for special education teachers.

Several times, I organized public hearings on the budget issues so that community members had the chance to voice their concerns about proposed cuts to programs. We did our best to keep all programs intact and keep our teachers fairly compensated, but there were some cuts to special education, our science resource program, and other supplemental programs by necessity. These decisions were based on thinking about what was in the best interest of the school as a whole. These are the kinds of decisions that cause a principal to lose sleep at night.

Charter schools are required to have a financial audit every year to ensure that public funds are being used appropriately. Under the leadership of Financial Officer Jane

Wofford, we began to use the information from our annual financial audit to continue to improve our accounting processes over time. Most years, we received no unsatisfactory comments and no findings from the auditor. However, when there were relatively minor comments, we moved decisively to improve our practice. The goal was to have financial audits that were free of any comments.

There were two areas of financial responsibility where we fumbled around and made lots of mistakes. These mistakes could have been avoided if we had known then what we know now. Those mistakes involved two entities that were tied to the school, but operated somewhat independently—the extended day program (EDP) and the parent organization.

From the beginning, we decided that EDP was part of the school. However, due to the overwhelming tasks involved with starting a new charter school, we allowed EDP to operate as a separate entity. The EDP coordinator set the fees, the budget, the programming, and hired her own staff. Although her finances ran through the school bank account, she was not initially required to adhere to the same accounting procedures and program protocols as the rest of the school. She ran a magnificent educational program and did a very good job of managing her finances. In the early days of the school, before the "great recession," attendance was high in EDP and the program was swimming in money. The EDP coordinator had more resources to spend than our classroom teachers. Later, as the attendance decreased, there were some deficit years. We did not think that money from the main educational program should subsidize EDP; rather, it should be the other way around.

When our auditor recommended that EDP use the same accounting practices as the rest of the school and be a part of the annual audit, we began to develop EDP financial policies. EDP now uses the same accounting procedures as the rest of the school. In addition, 12 percent of EDP revenue goes to the school to cover facility maintenance, repairs, electrical use, and custodial services for the program. My recommendation to new charter schools is to set up EDP from the beginning to include standard accounting procedures, administrative oversight, a standard percentage of revenue to cover facility costs, and a budget process with any EDP "profits" going back to the school's operating budget. EDP can be set up to be a financial asset for the school while providing parents affordable child care before and after school.

Just as we learned from our mistakes with EDP, we also learned a lot from mistakes that we made with the parent organization. In the early days of our school, the parent organization operated solely outside of the school's finances. They maintained their own checkbook and were not a part of the annual school audit. Later on, it was pointed out to us by the auditor that because they used the school's tax exempt number that the school was responsible for ensuring their accountability. It was logical that we proceeded to require that the parent organization keep their funds in an internal account in the school's budget so that it would be a part of the annual audit. Using an internal account, the parent organization still had complete control over the expenditure of those funds. However, they chose to see this as some kind of power grab by the school.

Based on these hard feelings, the officers of the parent organization reacted by joining the national PTA organization. As a separate organization, they applied for their own 501(c)(3) status, opened their own bank account, and got their own tax-exempt number. While they had a perfect right to do so, this has created a lot of extra work for subsequent officers who wonder why they have to maintain a lot of paperwork when they could easily just go through the school budget while retaining the same autonomy as an organization and access to their funds. My advice for new charter schools is that you set up an internal account for the parent organization from the very beginning and leave it that way.

Financial responsibility is one of the main characteristics of a successful charter school. When I served on the Charter School Appeals Commission, nothing caused a charter school's appeal to be rejected faster than financial irresponsibility. Sometimes charter school operators who are educators fail in this aspect of leadership because finances don't interest them. The fact is that running a charter school is more than managing an educational program; you have to run a business and think like an entrepreneur without letting the educational program suffer.

Chapter 9: Collaborative Leadership

A good leader does not do the thinking for the group, but elicits and assembles the best thinking of all group members, integrates it into a complete program, and communicates it to the group well enough to secure their acceptance of it. This is difficult but possible to do. To do the thinking for the group is not possible.　　　　—Harvey Jackins

Good leadership is absolutely necessary for a good school. Not just leadership from the principal and administrative team, but a "leadership culture" where everyone is expected to use their thinking to help the school improve. In a leadership culture, every person sees themselves as an important part of the school's success. Under good leadership, people are given many opportunities to develop new ideas and lead groups. There is a sense of openness and partnership. All staff members are treated with respect as professionals and are not micromanaged as long as they are on track with the school's mission and philosophy. Everyone is encouraged to take initiative—to start committees and study groups or propose new policies or procedures for the school. In any school, there are always things that need to be thought about, developed, and created. A school leader who empowers the teachers to take initiative is a school where ideas move forward and where teachers feel valued and engaged. It is the responsibility of the principal to set the tone for a leadership culture.

In our school, there is an expectation that everyone is a leader. Our faculty meetings are called "Teacher Leadership Council" or TLC. Although the principal facilitates these meetings, there is often the sharing of information among teachers or training led by teachers. In addition, there are small or large group discussions to solicit the teacher's ideas. Teacher-led committees are started from time-to-time as the need arises.

Every teacher is on an academic team. We have six teams: kindergarten and first grade teachers, second and third grade teachers, fourth and fifth grade teachers, sixth through eighth grade teachers, special area teachers (art, music, etc), and special education. Team leaders are chosen by the principal based on their experience and their organizational and leadership skills. Elementary teams meet bi-weekly while the middle school team meets weekly. The special area and special education teams meet as needed. All of the grade-level team leaders meet in a group with the principal, assistant principal, and guidance counselor every other week as the school's leadership team. This group discusses school issues and sets the agenda for the TLC meetings. Team leaders take ideas back to their teams, solicit feedback from them, and bring those ideas to the leadership team.

Teachers have many other kinds of leadership roles in the school. A good example of this is the numerous teacher-led study groups. These groups focus on specific academic areas or teaching practices. Teachers often organize a book study where they agree to read the same professional book and get together to discuss how they are implementing the ideas. Teachers are encouraged to start any groups that will help with their professional development.

Teachers are the backbone of any school. Hiring, supporting, and developing good teachers are some of the most important jobs of a school administrator. It is important to the mission of our school to find teachers whose educational philosophy is compatible with our school mission and who are willing to do the hard work of developing thematic, hands-on curriculum.

The selection process for teachers at our school is rigorous. First, applicants are screened by the principal who is not only looking at qualifications and experience, but educational philosophy, energy and enthusiasm, openness to new ideas, and ability to connect with other people. The principal brings a handful of the best applicants to the interview committee that is made up of at least one teacher, one parent, and one student. There are usually many teachers on the interview team. For instance, if a kindergarten and first grade lead teacher is being hired, usually the entire kindergarten and first grade team is on the interview panel because they will all be working closely with the new teacher.

The interview team, along with the principal, meets and interviews the top candidates. Discussion follows the interviews and the team makes its recommendations to the principal, who contacts the candidate's references and makes the final decision. This hiring process, which relies heavily on teacher input, is very important in empowering the teachers. Not only do empowered teachers feel more invested in the school and its mission, but a school leader is remiss if he or she does not take advantage of the knowledge and experience of teachers when making big decisions. Ninety-five percent of the time, the principal hires the person that the team recommends, but there are times when the principal has to exercise judgment based on other information.

I struggled with my power to hire and fire. Many times I held on to people for too long rather than terminating their employment at the end of a school year. There were instances where this leniency was not in the best interest of the school. Mainly this was because of a heightened sense of compassion for the individuals involved, as well as my propensity to want to be liked. I struggled with these two things while trying to do my best thinking about the school. There were times when I gave in to the desires of the interview team rather than follow my own thinking about a candidate for a job. When I caved to pressure and didn't follow my best thinking, I was usually displeased with the results. I learned from these experiences. A few times, I went against the advice of the interview team and followed my own thinking. I can honestly say that in one such case, even though some staff members were momentarily disgruntled with my decision, it was one of the best hires that I ever made.

As the years went by and I gained more experience, I learned how to spot the kind of educators that we needed for our school. When a graduate student interviewed me for a study about what factors principals consider in hiring teachers, I realized that what I looked for was different from most. I noticed that before deciding whom the interview committee would interview I always had a face-to-face interview with every candidate that met the criteria because what I was looking for could not be found on a resume. Many wonderful teachers with great credentials applied for jobs at our school, but I was looking for a spark, an excitement about life, an ability to connect with another person, a positive outlook, and enthusiasm about the subjects he or she would be teaching. I needed to look an applicant in the eye and just chat for a while to see if they met my criteria. I could usually tell in the first few minutes. If an applicant put me to sleep, I figured that they would do the same thing to their students. The second thing that I looked for in a teacher was passion for the learning process, the ability to innovate, the courage to try new things, and the confidence to think outside the box. We had an innovative curriculum and this required a certain type of teacher to be successful.

The result of my criteria was that I had a faculty that was very passionate about education and also very outspoken.

I wanted teachers who could see problems and take initiative to solve them. I learned that if I was going to hire teachers with strong personalities, I had to be willing to listen and synthesize a lot of their ideas. We were a much better school because the teachers were so committed to thinking outside the box.

Having a friendly, welcoming, efficient office staff is also crucial for a successful school. The people in the front office give the first impression of the school to visitors on campus. Training the office staff and treating them as professionals who know their job is important. Good leadership is seeing that things go well and this is the leadership function that the office staff performs for the school. A good office staff knows that the most important thing on campus is what is happening in the classrooms. Every effort needs to be made to support the classrooms, such as keeping classroom interruptions to a minimum and helping teachers who are preparing materials during planning periods.

*****

Encouraging leadership among students and parents is also important. Our weekly student council meetings are an opportunity to inform student leaders about school issues and get their input. Students are encouraged to develop their leadership skills in a variety of ways in their classroom activities, on stage, and on school committees. Parents also have many opportunities to participate in school activities and decisions. We always have a very active parent organization that raises money for the school and is responsible for many improvements on the property. In addition, we have a school advisory council (SAC) that has three teachers, three students, three parents, a support staff member, a board member, and the principal. The main responsibility of SAC is to write the school improvement plan which includes goals, strategies, and implementation for the following year. SAC also chooses three out of the seven members of the nominating committee which interviews potential board members and recommends who should be elected.

Parents who have children attending our school make up almost half of the membership on our board of directors. This gives a place in the highest level of school decision-making to parents. The foresight of one of the school's founders, Dr. Carolyn Schluck, resulted in a school policy that states that no more than 50 percent of the board can be parents. This has given us a board whose perspective is balanced between parents who have children attending the school and people from the wider community who do not have children attending the school. Parents tend to look at how school issues will affect their children while community members tend to see school issues in a bigger picture. This gives our board a broad, balanced perspective.

In a charter school, having good people serve on the board of directors is crucial to the success of the school. Our school has worked hard to attract competent board members who think clearly and are committed to the school's mission. People are recruited to run for the board who have specific skills that the board needs, such as financial, legal, or fundraising experience. The board's job is to set policies, hire and evaluate the principal, oversee the finances, and plan for the present and future needs of the school. An effective board is one that understands the difference between their role and that of the principal. A founding board who is trying to get a new school launched will often struggle to differentiate these roles. Ours certainly did. Our founding board held on to certain jobs that should have been the purview of the principal, such as final approval in the hiring process. Over time, our founding board became a professional board. A professional board will hire a good principal and leave the day-to-day operations of the school to him or her. A good board will be supportive of the principal while having high expectations for this leader's performance. Boards that micromanage the principal, or undermine his or her leadership in the school, are not operating in the best interest of the school.

At our school, board members are elected for a three-year term. Roughly one-third of the board seats are open for election each year. The board selection process begins with a prospective board member completing a board application. We generally have many more applicants than seats available. A nominating committee made up of four current board members and three members of the school advisory council (a parent, a student, and a teacher) interviews all of the applicants. After the interviews, the nominating committee recommends a list of candidates to the board. The board has the final vote.

In an independent charter school (one that does not rely on a management company), the board has tremendous power. I would caution charter school principals to not leave the recruiting of good board members to chance. Thinking about people outside the school community who would make good board members and asking them to apply is an important task for a charter school principal. Having proven community leaders who can think clearly in a crisis is imperative. Although I was not involved in the process for choosing board members, I took an active role in recruiting candidates for the board. Our board evolved in competence over time as it learned more about effective governance. It is important that the knowledge and insights that are learned get passed along to new board members. It is too easy for a board to devolve otherwise.

In my opinion, the most crucial relationship within the school is that between the board chair and the principal. Many charter schools have floundered because this relationship tends to be fraught with power struggles. I was lucky to have had a string of board chairs who were partners with me in improving the school. I say "lucky" because there were a few times in our history when the difference between having a supportive board chair or an obstreperous board chair was one vote difference. If the vote had gone another way, it is very possible that we would not have become the school that we did.

One thing that I did to facilitate a good working relationship with the board chair was to meet in person or by telephone often to keep him or her informed about the issues facing the school. This kind of open communication resulted in the development of problem-solving relationships that paid off in times of crisis.

In the first year that I was principal before our school opened, I spent one week at a new charter school outside of Boston to learn whatever I could from them. The school was a delightful place and the principal was an enthusiastic and dedicated woman who had founded the school. Unfortunately, there was quite a bit of friction between her and the board chair. I followed this school's progress for several years until it was destroyed by power struggles between the principal and the board chair. Even under the best of circumstances, starting and operating a charter school is difficult. Unless there is unity of purpose and support for the leader who is carrying the burden, the project is doomed. Our school, as a whole, and I, personally, owe a great debt to the courageous women and men who have served as the chair of our board of directors and have supported my leadership through hard times and great times.

In addition to the board chair, a principal should build open, trusting relationships with board members so that they feel free to communicate any concerns with the principal directly. At the beginning of each new school year, I invited all new board members to a special school tour in order to talk about and show the school's educational philosophy by visiting classrooms. This was one way that new board members could better understand what made our school different, as well as let them see my enthusiasm and passion about what we were creating. Just as the teachers and staff members had an "open door" to me, I wanted the board members to have that too. I invited them to contact me at any time about any concerns that they had.

Everything that happens in a school is the responsibility of the principal and a reflection on his or her leadership. Therefore, building an educational team through the hiring, training, supervision, and occasionally firing the people who make up that team is an important process in creating an outstanding school. In a charter school, all employees are hired for one year and are reappointed or let go at the end of that year. While many think that this is unfair and does not provide job security for employees, it tends to create a climate of excellence. While firing an employee can be one of the most painful things that a school leader must do, these decisions must be made in the best interest of the school's mission and the students, while being respectful to the person who needs to go. Not every person has the skills or the desire to work in an academic setting that requires as much time, energy, and creativity as our school. If a person's philosophy or time constraints are not compatible with the school and its mission, that usually becomes obvious and discussions can happen about what is best for the school and the individual. Having a good teacher evaluation process that the teachers help to develop can help make the process fair and effective.

Likewise, principals serve at the will of the board. Having a good evaluation system for the principal is necessary. The board of directors should hold the principal accountable for everything that is happening in the school. These standards and expectations should be communicated to the principal by the board before the beginning of the school year. At the end of each year, the principal should have the opportunity to present evidence that these standards and expectations were met. The board should give the principal feedback on what she did well and where she needs to improve. At our school, the principal's contract is for two years and has to be renewed after that time. However, there is an annual formal evaluation.

By the time our school had reached its "maturing years," we had developed an excellent system of evaluation for both teachers and the principal that includes a portfolio. Self-reflection is a big part of the process, as well as citing evidence of progress and feedback from those who evaluate. Both teachers and the principal set goals for the next year and these are revisited as part of the evaluation process. The purpose of an evaluation process is to encourage growth.

School administrators are expected to work all year long. As exciting as the job is, this is a difficult transition for a former teacher who has had summer downtime throughout her career. Teachers need their summer downtime to rest and refresh their minds for a new school year full of lesson plans and challenges with young people and parents. They need this time to rejuvenate and maintain their mental flexibility, as well as to generate new, creative ideas. Administrators need downtime too. They need an escape from the weight of the responsibilities that they carry. When the board of directors first hired me, I negotiated an eleven-month contract with them. This not only met my need to have time to go to Montana during the summer, but it saved the school money which was equally as important. Over the years, I had to struggle with my board to keep what felt like a necessity to me. Eventually, even though I was a twelve-month employee, there were enough vacation days in my contract for me to get time in Montana during the summer. Luckily, my school needed me enough to work out this arrangement with me. I believed that I paid back the school by working long hours during the school year. However, once I retired the next principal's contract did not include a big block of summer wilderness time. I remain forever grateful that I was allowed this consideration.

My leadership style is one based in collaboration and connection. I am not a top-down type of leader. I want people to be with me in the process of running the school, to share their thinking, and help mold the solutions to problems. The process of involving the thinking of others strengthens the final solution and produces a feeling of ownership. I think that this type of leadership style works best for charter schools, especially in those where a major goal is the empowerment of teachers and parents. Of course, there are some issues that need collaborative effort and others that need to just be handled by the school leader. Figuring which issues fall into which category is a continual learning process for a school leader.

One of the things that I noticed as the principal was that many times I was more focused on doing and accomplishing things than on the people around me. My mind would be so filled with issues and problems to solve that I would sometimes rush by people during the school day without really seeing them. I had to constantly remind myself to slow down and notice people and remember that any good project is based on relationships. I had to battle feelings of being alone with all of my responsibilities and notice that I was in this project with other people who were also working hard to make good things happen.

One thing that I learned from being a school leader is that new ideas bring up feelings in people. People want change; they want things to move forward, but change often makes people uncomfortable. I have noticed that a leader needs to have patience and allow people to work through their feelings before unity can be achieved. I remember one such issue relating to the class size amendment. Florida voters had approved by referendum an amendment to the Florida Constitution that classes in public schools be limited to a certain size. This threw us into a panic because although our elementary classrooms had two teachers (lead and associate) with twenty-six students, in the early days of our school the associate teachers were not required to hold a teaching certificate. About half of them were certified and half were not. The lead teacher was always certified, but on paper this looked like a 26:1 student-teacher ratio in classrooms where the associate was not certified.

I told the teachers that I thought that we would eventually need to have all of our associate teachers certified which would give us a 13:1 student-teacher ratio in our elementary classrooms. This would easily meet the requirements of the amendment (18:1 for grades kindergarten through third grade and 22:1 for grades four through eight). Offering this solution caused a great deal of turmoil among the staff because a few of our best associate teachers were going to be out of a job unless they could find a path to teacher certification. (For example, one such associate teacher was from another country and her college degree was not accepted by the Florida Department of Education, so although she was a superb teacher and had the qualifications to be one, there was no easy path for her.)

Teachers met to talk about the issue and there were a lot of feelings. Some people were furious with me for suggesting this proposal. I encouraged them to come up with another solution that would adhere to the new state requirements. I let the issue drop for a while because luckily, we had a few years to comply. This gave us time to replace uncertified associate teachers with certified ones as they left the school for various reasons. No one was fired because of this change and the teachers began to see how this solution was reasonable. In addition, the Department of Education eventually ruled that charter schools would be held to a school average rather than a class-by-class number and we could easily comply with this requirement.

I tell this story to point out that a school leader must expect reaction when new ideas are introduced. Under a traditional leadership structure, what the principal says is how it will be. Working with a collaborative model, the process is slower but the results are often better. When there is time to deliberate, giving your team the opportunity to work through their feelings about a proposed solution and leaving the door open for other possible solutions will eventually lead to unity. When there is unity and agreement around a change, things go better than dictatorial decisions. In addition, collaboration often produces a better solution.

I have also noticed that sometimes you have to present a new idea many times in a relaxed way before it catches on. For instance, you present an idea at a staff meeting and listen to the reactions. People think about it for weeks, maybe months. You raise the idea again and people react again. The idea percolates in their minds for another period of time. This may happen several times. Then, all of a sudden in a later discussion, the group comes up with your solution as though it were theirs. Sometimes they have even forgotten that you originally raised the idea. That's OK. President Harry S.

Truman said it best when he declared, "It is amazing what you can accomplish if you do not care who gets the credit."

I believe that school leaders need to build an organization that is not based on themselves. One of the jobs of a good leader is to be constantly training and supporting other people's leadership. I knew that when I retired, I wanted the school to continue to move forward and thrive without me. A good leader offers many leadership opportunities for everyone in the organization. As the school leader, I tried to be aware of who stood out and give that person encouragement to take on larger leadership. I understood that a good leader begins to train her replacement long before he or she leaves the organization, so I started that process many years before I even knew when I would be retiring. The result was a very smooth transition.

Even in a school with a leadership culture, there is one person who sets the tone for the whole community and that is the principal. The role of the principal is spelled out in school policy, but it is more than that. Basically, the principal has to think about the whole school and take responsibility for moving things forward. The principal is hired by the board, annually evaluated by the board, and is ultimately answerable to the board, but this person is the visible leader of the school and has a lot of power over its direction. This power is more than decision making power; it is more a spiritual thing. The principal breathes into a school its spirit, its passion, and its inspiration. Before becoming a principal, I often led workshops for teachers in schools across the state of Florida. In my first five to ten minutes with these teachers, I could tell what kind of principal their school had because the teachers reflected the attitude of the school's leadership.

As educators, we know that students learn best in an environment where they feel valued and respected and safe. Just as good teachers create this environment in their classrooms, good principals create this environment in their schools. A principal who is enthusiastic about the school's mission, open and positive with everyone on campus, and hopeful about the future, can do what I call "leading by attitude." A relaxed, hopeful tone from the principal is contagious.

In order to stay relaxed and hopeful in the face of all of the worries, concerns, problems, dramas, and crises in a school, a principal needs a place to vent frustrations, fears, and insecurities, as well as a place to talk through issues. It is helpful if the principal has a support team or support person outside of the school. Many principals use a spouse, a friend, another principal, a counselor, or a support group as a place to show the feelings that sometimes tend to engulf us and cloud our thinking. The result of this process is clearer thinking, more confidence, and the ability to model a positive attitude for the school. This is not only emotionally healthy behavior for the Principal, but is a benefit for the entire school.

My support team was an army of co-counselors, locally and around the world, with whom I could trade listening time.

I used listening exchanges with these co-counselors by phone if they lived in distant places or in person if they lived locally. These co-counselors are leaders in other areas of the community outside of our school, and they need to be listened to also. I listen to them for a designated amount of time and they listen to me for the same amount of time. Having a confidential place to take my own feelings makes it possible for me to set these feelings aside and listen more openly to other people at my school and in the rest of my life. The process of co-counseling helped me to clear all of the feelings of discouragement, exhaustion, inadequacy, worry, fear, and doubt so that I could hold out a positive tone for the school no matter what crisis we were facing.

Sometimes, I would spend two minutes in my office yawning deeply before a potentially tense meeting. Contrary to popular notions about yawning, brain scientists are discovering that yawning serves many purposes in "waking up the brain." Yawning brings more oxygen to the brain and brings a person into mental alertness by increasing brain chemicals, called neurotransmitters, such as GABA, serotonin, and acetylcholine. Taking time to yawn before meetings helped to relieve tension, relax me, and restore my naturally positive attitude before entering a meeting.

The principal has the power to set the tone for the school. This power cannot be minimized. It is more important than advanced degrees, years of experience, and any amount of training. My gift to our school was my energy and enthusiasm, my passion for our school's mission, my hopefulness about the future, and my belief that we could do it.

Section III: The Supports

Chapter 10: Building a Leadership Culture

A school with a leadership culture is characterized by an expectation that everyone is a leader; that everyone has a leadership role to play to make the school the best that it can be. In a leadership culture, there are eight skills that need to be taught:

1. **Listening Skills**. It is much easier to talk than to listen. In fact, because we all need to be listened to so much, often we are all talking and no one is really listening. A good leader is one who can listen to other people's ideas and opinions with respect and an open mind. Putting aside one's own feelings and opinions is sometimes a difficult task, but a good leader can choose to do that in order to elicit other people's thinking. As the guidance counselor at our school is fond of reminding us: everyone wants to be right! To be a good listener, we must set aside our need to be right, at least for a few moments. By listening, we can learn new

things and expand our thinking in many areas. The mere act of listening to someone helps them to organize their thoughts, separate their thoughts from their feelings, and can often lead to a reevaluation or clarification of a person's thinking. Listening skills, like any other skill, have to be practiced and improved upon. Teachers at our school have used various techniques to develop their listening skills, including "listening exchanges" where a pair takes turns talking and listening. This technique has been used in faculty meetings to share thinking about various topics or to just talk about one's day before the meeting starts. Listening exchanges can also be used when two staff members need to work out a conflict or misunderstanding. The principal provides the model for the school's listening skills. It was important to me to have an open door policy which created many interruptions in my day, but made it obvious to the teachers and staff that I always had time to listen to their concerns. When someone came to my door, I would stop what I was working on and give my full attention to them. As a result, there was sometimes a line of people outside my door waiting to talk. Although this often meant staying at school late to catch up on work that got postponed, taking time to listen to teachers and staff was one of my most important and enjoyable roles as the principal. What I learned was that listening is an excellent method for diffusing upset feelings. I cannot count the times when an angry parent or teacher came to my office. When I gave them my attention and calmly listened, they would eventually calm down. After having a chance to express their feelings vehemently, they would start thinking clearly again and solutions would start to present themselves. This phenomenon is typical of most human beings. When we get upset, our feelings cloud our thinking. If we are given the chance to spew out the feelings with a good listener who will not take offense, our minds start to function rationally again. The skill of listening is the most important tool in a principal's leadership arsenal. To go a step further, for leaders to be able to be relaxed listeners when someone is venting their feelings, they need to have a place where they can be listened to also. One time an angry parent came to my office to talk about her son. I listened to her thoroughly, and when she wound down, I smiled brightly at her and said, "I'm so glad to meet a parent who really loves her son and wants what is best for him!" This seemed to take all of the "fight" out of her and we proceeded to have a productive conversation about her son and what could be done to support him.

2. **Seeing the Difference Between Feelings and Thinking.** These get very confused because we often talk about them as though they are one and the same. As human beings, we all have feelings. Feelings are not

bad, they are just feelings. However, feelings can sometimes cloud our good judgment and our best thinking. It is important for a leader to be able to identify the difference between feelings and thinking. Feelings can be validated and listened to with respect, but they are not a good guide for taking action. It is best if a leader can listen to someone's feelings until they dissipate to the point that their thinking gets clearer. An example is when a new initiative is introduced which will change something in the school. Change initiates feelings. Even if the change is beneficial to everyone, it spawns feelings. It is important for a leader to remember that change is always accompanied by feelings. If a leader expects this and is not upset or scared by this, he or she can listen to the feelings in a relaxed way that will help the group move forward and accept the change.

3. **Genuinely Liking People and Seeing Their Goodness**. The truth is that sometimes people can be difficult to like. The key is to see the goodness in each person and treat them with complete respect, no matter how they behave. When I treat people this way, they most often rise to the occasion. I believe that people are inherently good, intelligent, and loving and yearn to be seen in this way. Making a distinction between the person and their behavior is important. Good teachers do this all of the time. Although they don't always like their behavior, they care deeply about their students. An

effective teacher knows that there is a difference between a student and his or her misbehavior. That teacher will reach for a connection with the misbehaving student rather than just punishing the behavior. This is not to say that there are not consequences for inappropriate behavior; however, to avoid future problems, there has to be a human-to-human connection developed between the teacher and the student. This is just as true for adult interactions. Seeing the angry parent as a person who loves their child and someone who is a potential ally in the student's education can move the situation forward to a productive place.

4. **The Power of Appreciation**. People yearn to be recognized for the good things that they do. None of us are ever appreciated enough, particularly teachers who give so much of themselves every day. A good leader will notice and recognize people's efforts. The art of appreciating people effectively is a skill that can be learned. At our school, teachers teach students how to appreciate each other. In addition, we set up time for teachers to appreciate each other at the beginning of faculty meetings. As a principal, I regularly acknowledge people publicly in meetings and morning announcements, as well as personally. A little appreciation and recognition builds self-esteem, confidence, motivation, and positive attitudes. Besides

that, it is the way that people should just naturally act toward each other.

5. **Mistakes Are OK**. Mistakes are an inherent part of the learning process. If someone is doing something challenging or new, making mistakes is inevitable. We learn from our mistakes. Most of us were punished as children for making mistakes, so we try to avoid them by being too careful, and when mistakes happen, we try to deny or cover them up. Sometimes we defend them and try to convince others that they really weren't mistakes at all. Actually, the proper course for a leader who has made a mistake is to admit it and move quickly to correct the mistake. A leader, who is honest about their mistakes without being sloppily remorseful, is a model for everyone. An example is saying to the faculty: "I made a mistake. I moved us in a direction that seemed like it was the best for the school, but it wasn't, so now we are going to change course."

6. **Backing the Leader**. Even in the most inclusive group where everyone's thinking is taken into account, there is a point at which the group needs to move on. Sometimes, after discussion and input, the leader needs to make the final decision and the group needs to back the leader. I remember a faculty meeting where I reminded the teachers, who were predominantly women, how difficult it is for women to back a woman leader. Because women are the targets of sexism in our society,

we have internalized the messages about other women and sometimes don't trust each other. I told the faculty that we could discuss and disagree and I would take all of their ideas into consideration, but when it was time for the final decision, I needed them to back me. This was a good reminder to all of us and things worked much better after that. One teacher who often disagreed with me in discussions, thanked me for asking them to back me, and our relationship grew as a result. Knowing when it is time to disagree and when it is time to move on is an important skill for any collaborative group to have. I firmly believe that you can't be a good leader unless you know how to back leadership.

7. **Training Other Leaders**. Whatever our role, we should always be training our replacement. With this in mind, there will never be a leadership vacuum because someone will be ready to step in if something happens to the leader. At our school, lead teachers are training their associates and the principal is training her assistant. Parent leaders share information and train the new parent leaders. Board members train new board members. A leadership culture requires the passing on of important skills and information.

8. **Taking Care of Your Self.** When one is working hard for long hours, it is easy to burn out. Steps can be taken to minimize this. Leaders need to value their health and prioritize the time to take care of themselves

in their busy schedules. Leaders need to be well rested, well nourished, and well exercised. Many educators tend to be overweight and exhausted because of long hours working. After working at school, many go home to care for families and work on their lesson plans. At our school, we focus on wellness. At the beginning of staff meetings, we often have listening exchanges to share what we have been doing to take care of ourselves. There have been yoga classes and walking groups after school. Teachers make appointments with the school counselor when they have emotional issues. In our rush to fill our days with meaningful ways to make the world better or just do our jobs well, we often neglect ourselves. A good leader must take time to stay healthy. This will make him or her more effective as a leader. Educators should never be blamed for having a hard time figuring out how to get enough exercise. The demands of the job, coupled with the demands of family, usually take up all of the minutes in a day. I found myself in the same bind as many educators. I worked long hours and went home to take care of household chores and my daughter. In later years, she was living on her own and I had fewer parental responsibilities. Not until that point did I figure out how to put exercise back into my schedule. I went to the gym before school two to three times a week for a hard aerobic workout. After working a long day, I often went to a dance class. I knew that after being inside my head all day, I needed to be inside my body for a while. This greatly improved my health and my ability to do my job and I did my best to model this for the rest of the staff.

Creating a school that belonged to all of us was important in our vision for the school and for the world as a whole. Because of this ideal, we did not utilize a typical top-down type of leadership model. We wanted everyone in the school community to feel like it was their school and they played an important role as a leader. We found that teaching these eight skills went a long way toward creating a leadership culture at our school.

Every time we tackled an issue where there was disagreement, we used these eight skills. We would provide forums for different ideas to be expressed and we listened to each other thoroughly with respect (skill one). We noticed when someone was expressing their feelings or their thinking and we tried to remember to separate the two things (skill two). We knew that we liked and cared about each other even when we did not agree about a particular issue (skill three). We appreciated a person's hard work and good intentions even if we disagreed with their ideas (skill four). We were not critical when mistakes were made rather we thought about what had been learned from the experience and how we could do better in the future (skill five). After lots of hard work on an issue, we backed the final decision (skill six). We shared information and skills with each other rather than hoarding these in an attempt to maintain power over others (skill seven). And, lastly, we valued and took care of ourselves (skill eight).

Obviously, we were not able to do all of these things all of the time, but this was the model that we strived for in our interactions with each other. As a result, we had a picture of how cooperatively the world can function when everyone does their part.

Chapter 11: Empowering Teachers

Teachers are the heroes and heroines of our society.

You cannot have a good school without good teachers. Teachers do some of the world's most important work: educating the next generation of citizens and leaders. They work countless hours beyond the school day thinking, planning, and developing lessons and activities for their students. In most places, they are underpaid for the work that they do. On top of that, they are usually blamed for the failings of the educational system.

Most teachers come into the profession because they love learning and they want to make a difference. They have a vision for how things will be in their classroom. The beginning of an academic year in a school is the most hopeful place to be on the planet. Teachers start every school year hopeful that they will be able to attain their vision, that great things will happen in their classrooms. They are energized and ready to meet their new students. Teachers are some of the most optimistic and hopeful people that I know. They begin every new school year as a fresh new beginning. At that point, it feels like nothing can stop them.

However, within a few months, the discouragement starts to sets in. There are a million things that get in the way of achieving their vision, but mainly it boils down to not enough time and not enough attention for the large numbers of young people in their care. This is not their failing, although they usually feel that it is. Rather, this is the failing of our system of education that expects mere humans to create miracles with not enough time for planning and thinking, not enough classroom resources, and certainly not enough compensation.

And yet, despite these deficiencies, teachers **do** create miracles. They come to school every day and work their hardest to meet the needs of their students. No matter how they are feeling or what else is happening in their lives, they manage a roomful of young people with varying abilities and desire to be there. There are not many people in other professions that are tested that strenuously day after day or could even handle the myriad of problems and situations that teachers confront as a matter of course.

Despite the miracles that they accomplish, teachers are blamed for the failures of our educational system. In our society, which is constantly looking for someone to blame, teachers are the target. As a result, legislatures devise all kinds of additional paperwork and bureaucratic nonsense that rates teachers against each other and adds to their workload. A good principal knows which teachers are the outstanding ones, the mediocre ones, and the ineffective ones. The outstanding ones should be given the resources they need to push to greater heights. The mediocre ones should receive encouragement and training to help them grow. The ineffective ones should be encouraged to find another profession.

Every teacher deserves our thanks and our appreciation for the work that they have chosen to do. Without them, our nation and our world would be a sorry place indeed. Any Educational System, Management Company, Board of Directors, or Principal who does not keep this foremost in their minds when developing a school is not going to be able to have an exemplary school. Schools are not factories and teachers are not commodities or cogs in the wheel; they are not workers to be exploited in a push for profit; they are certainly not the reason that our educational system has not reached its full potential. Teachers are actually the hope, the driving force, the potency behind a really good school...but only if they are empowered.

Teachers must be permitted to think, create, lead, and change things that are not working. Rather than be micromanaged and distrusted, teachers need to be set free to innovate and try new things, even if they make a few mistakes along the way.

How is this empowerment accomplished?

1. **Teachers must have a strong voice in how the school is run, what policies and procedures govern everyday life, and who is hired for positions within the school.** A principal who solicits the ideas of

teachers, listens, and uses the best ideas is a smart leader because the ideas of many are more powerful than the ideas of a few. At our school, teachers have the opportunity to voice their opinions on almost everything that happens in the school through team meetings, faculty meetings, and leadership meetings. They also serve on interview teams when we are hiring new staff members. When a teacher comes to my office with an idea, I stop what I am doing and listen to the idea. If I think that it is a good idea, we decide how best to proceed. If I don't agree, we discuss an avenue for broader discussion with the faculty. Teachers should feel free to talk to the principal directly.

2. **Teachers should be encouraged to lead on every issue that they find interesting.** For example, at our school, teachers lead book study groups, make presentations on successful teaching methods at the faculty meetings, or start committees to explore ideas for reform within the school. Giving teachers these opportunities can unleash a powerhouse of information and experience that will enrich the entire school program. An example from our school is the time that a teacher thought that the school should have a school-wide field day. She brought the idea up in her team meeting and the faculty meeting to get support and then started a committee to work on the details. The

committee organized the field day and it has become an annual event.

3. **Teachers should be treated as professional educators and encouraged to innovate and try new things.** For example, the middle school social studies teacher came to me to say that she was teaching about the industrial revolution in the United States, but the students had no idea what a sweatshop was. She asked, "Can I turn my classroom into a sweatshop for a day?" With my enthusiastic approval, she put dark paper over the windows to make the room dreary, ran space heaters to make it very hot and stuffy, and set the room up as a crowded shop where students had to do menial labor for fifteen minutes while she barked at them to work faster. After the simulation was over, the class discussion about sweatshops was animated and stimulating. I always encourage teachers to try new things in their classrooms and report back about what they learned. When teachers feel supported by the principal to innovate, exciting things happen in classrooms.

A good school is one where the teachers know that the school is theirs, where their identity is solidly linked to the school, where the success of the school is their own personal success. Nothing can substitute for this kind of connection. After my two decades in the classroom, I know that this is true.

And after spending more than a decade as a school administrator, I know that the following is true: *to have a school where the teachers are empowered is the responsibility of the principal.* He or she is the one who must set this tone by attitude and deed.

This is not to say that all teachers are great teachers. Every teacher at a school is at a different stage of development. A good administrator will know the strengths and weaknesses of each teacher and how to offer appreciation, encouragement, training, and resources to help each teacher continue to grow. A good administrator will also have to use judgment about which teachers to retain and which ones should not be rehired for the following year. Charter school principals have more leeway in this regard than do principals in district schools.

A good teacher evaluation process is necessary and most teachers want honest feedback on their performance. Yet, in an attempt to develop good teachers, some evaluation instruments are too cumbersome and lengthy. Some focus on the wrong things or too many things and leave teachers feeling worried, unseen, and under-appreciated for all of the hard work that they do. The best teachers are constantly evaluating themselves and their lessons and striving for improvement. They hold high standards for themselves and work hard to achieve them. A good principal knows who these star teachers are. They should be set free to innovate and try new things. They should be encouraged and allowed to focus on their teaching. On the other hand, developing teachers need more monitoring and feedback to help them improve.

Teachers should have a voice in developing the tools and processes that are used to evaluate them. A teacher's performance cannot be measured solely by the results of their student's standardized test scores. While student achievement is an important thing to measure in regards to teacher performance, there are many ways to measure this in addition to a standardized test score. There are also many qualities of good teaching that go beyond just getting students through a particular test.

At the School of Arts and Sciences, teachers are an integral part of the school management. They are respected, valued, listened to, and encouraged to take leadership and to innovate in their classrooms. Our teachers are the keys that unlock the potential in each of our students. Without their energy, enthusiasm, and commitment to excellence, we would not have an exemplary school.

Chapter 12: Eliminating Racism

No one is born hating another person because of the color of his skin, or his background, or his religion. People must learn to hate, and if they can learn to hate, they can be taught to love, for love comes more naturally to the human heart than it's opposite.
                                        --Nelson Mandela

The Civil Rights Movement was inspiring to me. As a white child growing up in the segregated South, I was glued to the TV set listening to Dr. King's speeches. Because the schools, churches, and neighborhoods of my childhood were segregated, I had few opportunities to work, play, socialize, and make friends with black children. I felt deprived and ignorant because of these circumstances; like I was somehow part of the problem. I was not the problem. The oppressive society that I was born into was the problem. I saw the "colored only" and "white only" signs on bathrooms, waiting rooms, and water fountains and found this troubling. Watching the brutality aimed at black people as it was reported on TV news, I horrified my mother by telling her that I was ashamed to be white. I saw people courageously and nonviolently facing hatred, anger, police dogs, and fire hoses and I felt like they were my people even though my skin color was different from most of theirs. I longed for a world where black and white children could be friends and classmates. I wasn't sure what a child could do to change the world, but I began to speak out in my school, church, and 4-H Club about racism. I could not be silent, even when classmates called me "n-lover" for liking President Kennedy and supporting civil rights. I insisted that my friends not use the "n-word" around me. I stood with my parents among the hostile stares of our friends and neighbors to vote in our white Southern Baptist church to open the church to anyone who wanted to attend regardless of race. It was the Civil Rights Movement that caused me to question how things were, demonstrated to me what courage looked like, and inspired me to dream about a better world.

My first chance to be in an integrated environment was at the 4-H State Congress in Gainesville where I was competing in public speaking. 4-H, as a part of the US Agricultural Extension Service, is a federally-funded operation and was mandated to integrate. The first year that white and black 4-H kids competed against each other, I gave a speech about ending racism. This instantly endeared me to the black students and I made some friends, one young man in particular. I could tell that we were making the adults around us very uncomfortable, but I persisted in being friendly with him despite the feeling that I was treading on dangerous ground. At the dance that evening, a girlfriend of mine and I danced with the black kids and immediately became the targets of wrath from our white 4-H adult leaders. We were probably triggering their worst fears and prejudices—white girls with black boys. It was probably the slow dance that kicked them over the edge. We were basically yanked off the floor and sent to our dorm where we organized a meeting of the other girls to share with them what had happened. We were righteously indignant about our treatment and spoke about it every chance we got. I think that we actually had some adult leaders who sympathized with our position, but they were too fearful to go against the majority.

While attending Pensacola Junior College, I worked with the "Now Party" made up of white and black students who organized to win the Student Government elections. As late as 1970, while returning from an anti-war rally in Tampa, a group of us traveling together were refused service in a restaurant in Perry, Florida because one of our group was black. I tell these stories not to reinforce the mistaken notion that the South is the only place that racism has existed, but to point out how far the South has come in my lifetime. That is something of which we can be proud.

During my intern teaching semester at Florida State University in 1973, I worked at a local high school and was assigned to a social studies teacher who taught US History to "advanced" students. During the weeks that I was in charge of all of her classes, we were studying the 1920s. Although the history textbook had very few references to the lives of people of African descent, I thought that it was important to include a lecture on segregation, Jim Crow laws, the Ku Klux Klan, and methods used to impede the voting rights of people of color. My supervising teacher did not interrupt my lesson; however, afterward she told me that there had been race riots at the school in previous years and the "students do not want to hear about all that stuff." Actually, the students had been quite interested in the class, but I did not point this out because it was clear to me that she was the one who was uncomfortable with the material. I wondered how we could ever expect anyone to change if there was no space to discuss and explore these issues and reach for understanding. In my mind it seemed like schools were one of the best places for this to happen.

After finishing college, I looked for a teaching job. It seemed impossible to get a job in Tallahassee as a first year teacher, so I was ecstatic when offered a job in Gadsden County adjacent to Leon County. After growing up in a rigidly segregated world, I taught for three years in a Gadsden County public middle school with about a 98 percent black student body. The reason for this percentage had its roots in the history of the county. Where there had formerly been white public schools and black public schools, this was no longer allowed when school desegregation was mandated. As a result, most of the white parents in the county had pulled their children from the public schools and enrolled them in private Christian schools leaving the public schools with mostly black students. Not only was the county divided along racial lines, but these divisions were similar to the socioeconomic divisions as well. Almost all of my students were very poor. Many of them were without health or dental care, wearing very shabby clothing, and reading way below grade level. It was culture shock for this young, idealistic white girl starting her first teaching job.

In the mid-70s, Gadsden County seemed like it was still locked in the paradigm of the Old South. Although the black population was in the majority, white people held all of the political power. Public schools were in terrible shape and given few resources. My analysis at the time was that they purposefully did not want to educate the majority black population. Things have changed a lot since then, but that was my impression at the time.

As with all first year teachers, I struggled to prepare lessons and settle into my own style of teaching and classroom management based on my philosophy and ideals. On top of my cultural ignorance about my students, the conditions were difficult. For instance, there were 39 to 40 middle school students in each of my five social studies classes. As a new teacher, I was assigned to the lowest level students, many of whom could not read. There was no air conditioning and a school year that started in early August when the temperature and humidity were close to 100. The school used corporal punishment that I opposed on philosophical grounds, but this was what the students expected when they misbehaved. Needless to say, my students initially walked all over me as I tried to implement a classroom based on mutual respect.

During the first semester, I scrambled to make my social studies classes relevant to them using textbooks that were boring, out-of-date, and beyond their reading abilities. I soon quit using the textbooks and developed my own lessons with materials that I had gathered in other places. I noticed that the self-esteem of the students was extremely low and reflected the way that they had been treated. I made the decision to engage them in self-esteem building activities and based my lessons on black history. I wanted them to be proud of who they were. By the second semester, my classroom walls were covered with student art featuring famous black historical figures. My students recognized that my classroom was a welcoming place for them where they wouldn't be yelled at or beaten. At times, we could hear students from other classrooms being paddled in the hallway outside our classroom. I made it clear that would not happen to them when they were with me. Over time, my classroom management improved as I developed trusting relationships with my students.

I learned a lot by being immersed in black culture for three years. I remember sitting in the bleachers in the school gym at a pep rally among a sea of black faces with the whole place swaying and singing as one big joyful group. It was exhilarating to be there and I realized the great gift that I had been given to be a respected member of this community despite my white skin. I loved my students; however, my heart was in innovative education and the school system where I was working was very stifling to creativity. After three years, I took a job as a social studies teacher at SAIL High School in Tallahassee. SAIL was one of the most innovative public schools in the nation and I was excited to be a part of it.

When I taught US History at SAIL High School, I used the thematic approach that I had developed at my former school. Having acquired a love for black history, I devoted an entire six weeks period to its study. In addition, I taught the history of Native Americans, Latino/as, Asians, and women since these groups are often minimized in a traditional study of US History.

In 1990, inspired by the work of Cheri Brown and her National Coalition Building Institute, I wrote two training manuals for the Florida Department of Education called "Celebrating Diversity" and "Ending Racism." I later became involved in a project called "United to End Racism" (UER) which teaches people how to heal from the hurts of racism. As a member of several multi-racial UER teams, I co-led workshops at conferences around the country. One such workshop was "Southerners Ending Racism." I also led a workshop locally for the Mayor's Race Relations Summit on "The Role of White People in Ending Racism." It was a great pleasure to work with people on this topic and see the difference that it made.

It is no wonder that when I was hired as the principal of the School of Arts and Sciences that I brought with me a desire for our school to become a force for the liberation of all people from oppressive attitudes and behaviors, especially racism.

There are at least three things that I know for sure about racism:

1. **No white person was born with racist attitudes and beliefs.** We came into the world as innocent children and were accosted by the emotional hurts and prejudices that the adults around us carried. As innocent children, we picked up some of these oppressive attitudes from the people around us. It was as though we were dipped into a vat of contamination and it left its residue on us. We are not to blame for this.

2. **All of us have been hurt by racism** whether or not we have been targeted by racism. In other words, racism hurts white people as well as people of color. One way this hurt manifests itself is in the isolation of white people from a majority of the world's population.

3. **We can heal from the hurts of racism.** Ending racism will require more than nondiscrimination laws and changing our institutions. We must change our hearts and minds. It is completely possible to "unlearn" racism.

How does racism hurt people? It is obvious how people of color have been targeted by racism throughout our country's history. This has taken every form from enslavement to brutal violence to institutional discrimination to insulting comments and attitudes. These hurts are internalized in individuals who are targeted by racism. The messages and misinformation perpetrated by racism are internalized and this affects how people of color think about themselves and each other. Internalized racism is directed inwardly toward oneself and outwardly toward members of a person's racial group. Internalized racism leaves people with feelings of inadequacy which can lead to limited functioning. It is easy to see how internalized racism can affect the success of students of color in schools.

What is less obvious to many people is how white people are hurt by racism. Every white person is affected in some way. Many white people carry guilt about what has been done to people of color by white people. Guilt gets in the way of being a strong and vocal ally to people who have been targeted with racism. Some white people blatantly act out oppressive attitudes while the rest of us distance ourselves from those white people and try to act like we don't have any of those feelings locked secretly inside of ourselves. We are the "good white people" after all. However, there are ways that we have all been contaminated by racism. Even when we work hard to hide it, it still eats away at us, affects our relationships, and shows up sometimes when we are not vigilant about keeping it hidden. Unaware racism on the part of white people is usually very obvious to people who have been targeted by racism. If these things are pointed out to us, we often get defensive about it because we work so hard to keep it hidden. Purging ourselves of racism is difficult if we can't even admit that it exists.

Racism can be eliminated. We, as a society, are not stuck in this forever. We can purge every vestige of this contamination from our minds. We can heal from the hurts of racism and create schools and communities where it is not allowed to operate.

Schools are important places where societal changes can occur. Schools can either be places where societal oppressions are reinforced or they can be places that stand for freedom and liberation from oppression. To do this, schools must be places where everyone is respected and encouraged to excel to their greatest ability. Schools must be safe enough for issues around oppression to be discussed and where we can learn to be allies for each other. There is so much that we can learn from each other and schools are great places for this to happen. Parents, students, and teachers need to be able to tell their stories to others who eagerly listen in order to gain understanding.

Before our school even opened, our thinking about how to have a racially, culturally, and socioeconomically diverse school population was important in laying the groundwork for our commitment to creating a climate of respect on our campus. We worked hard to attract a diverse population to our school and to create a climate of respect. Listening skills were taught and opportunities were offered so that people could learn from each other and celebrate the diversity of our community.

In the early years of our school, I met with the parents of students of color annually to ask questions and listen to them about how things were going for their children at our school. I learned a great deal in these interactions and developed good relationships with these parents. Many of these parents saw me as an ally who would listen respectfully to them. I asked them to be partners with the teachers in helping their children achieve.

Knowing that there is an achievement gap between students based on race, I led teacher training on issues around racism and oppression and how these things affect student achievement and learning. We analyzed standardized test data to develop specific plans for individual students who needed more resources. The entire faculty read and discussed William Jenkins' book called *Understanding and Educating African American Children* (William Jenkins Enterprise, 2004) and implemented many ideas from it. Early on, our teachers were committed to closing the achievement gap and this goal remains a focus to this day.

Parents were also involved in learning more about each other. One year, the parent organization sponsored a program where I led a diversity panel in January near the Martin Luther King, Jr. holiday. The panel was made up of parents who represented the wide diversity of our school community. It was a wonderful exchange of information and understanding. There were several rounds of questions:

--What is great about being (of African heritage, Asian heritage, Latino/a heritage, Middle Eastern heritage, born outside the United States, etc.)?

--What is hard about being (of African heritage, Asian heritage, Latino/a heritage, Middle Eastern heritage, born outside the United States, etc)?

--How has this school community been helpful to you and your family?

--How could our school community improve in its interactions with you and your family?

Another year, the parent organization sponsored an evening discussion on race, diversity, and the philosophy of Dr. Martin Luther King, Jr., which I facilitated. A process was used that gave parents the chance to share their thinking and feelings about (1) what inspired them about Dr. King's life and his work, (2) what part of his vision has been implemented at our school, and (3) where do we go from here to continue to build our relationships with each other across racial barriers.

In my childhood as I watched the Civil Rights conflicts, I thought that if the adults would just back off, the children could solve the problems by making connections with each other across racial lines. The children in those years are now parents and grandparents. Although it has taken decades for the change to happen, it can be seen every day on our school campus. When altercations did occur, I took the time to meet with the students who were involved in order to unravel and work through the issues. Many times, the tears and anger needed to be listened to before the students were able to reconnect with each other again.

One year, I led a support group for black mothers at our school who were interested in healing the hurts of racism. I met with these women on an evening every other week. There was time for each one to share stories of things that had happened to them during their lives. I offered my attention and it became a safe space for them despite the fact that I am white. There was much talking, crying, laughing, and raging. At times they even trusted me enough to let me stand in the place of every white person who had ever hurt them so that they could "tell me off." I could confidently and calmly listen to their feelings when I was with them because I was doing my own work in a different support group (off campus) for white people working on the hurts of racism.

My test came with a member of our staff. Although most of the time, she welcomed visitors, staff, and students with a friendliness and warmth that exemplified our school, there were days when she was mad at the world and it leaked out into her interactions with everyone. She was a very powerful black woman and people were sometimes scared of her. Sometimes there were scenes in the front office when she would get angry about something that someone did. In the privacy of my office, I told her that she could come into my office and yell and scream if something was bothering her, but she absolutely could not do it in the front office. Basically, I was offering her one-way counseling time when she needed it. I was committed to her and I knew that she carried a tremendous load of feelings about all of the racism that she had experienced during her life.

My invitation was accepted and she would sometimes just rage at me. Sometimes she accused me of trying to turn her into a white person. She told me that trying to create a place of respect was "not living in the real world." To me, this sounded like it came from all of the demeaning experiences in her past. She had been a target of racism so many times in her life that feelings of anger could easily be triggered by something in the present. Being in a place where respect was offered to her and expected from her was a major contradiction to the way she saw the world and protected herself from it. I saw her emotional outbursts with me as the result of the safety that had been established between us that allowed this healing to take place. I could not have listened to her in this way if I had not done my own work around racism for many years prior to this. As a result, I was able to stay relaxed and warm with her. We hung in there with each other and it brought us close together. Years later, she told me that I had "raised her." And, she told others that she raised me from a baby principal to an experienced one. I suppose we were both right. We raised each other.

White people have a major role to play in the ending of racism. To be an effective ally and have good relationships with people of color, we have to be committed to working on all of the ways that our minds have been distorted by living in a society where racism exists. As we work on ourselves, our relationships improve.

Racism is not the only oppression that operates in our society and our schools, but it is a key issue that can make a major difference if it is addressed. Schools exist within the framework of an oppressive society where every person receives negative messages about who they are based on age, gender, race, socioeconomic status, religion, body type, sexual orientation, nationality, and many other identities. These negative messages affect the learning process. Schools can be places of liberation where these negative messages are contradicted. For instance, because girls tend to show fewer propensities toward science than boys, our middle school science teacher organized a girl's science camp in the summer. Another example was having special events in classrooms where our international students and their parents had the opportunity to share their culture in an atmosphere of complete respect.

One way to make our society better is to make our schools better. Schools can lead the way in creating a world of peace and prosperity for all. Learning environments can be created where each student and teacher is valued and encouraged to reach for their highest dreams despite the negative messages that have been internalized.

Chapter 13: Handling Attacks on the Leader

By far, the hardest thing for me as the school leader was the attacks that a few people perpetrated. I knew from my years of teaching leadership development workshops that leaders often become targets. In fact, I had witnessed it happening to other leaders in the various organizations in which I was involved before the school. I noticed how often people inexplicably undermined the work of the organization by going after the leader. This hostile climate for leadership development is why so many people are unwilling to take on a major leadership role.

An important skill for a principal is to be able to listen to criticism and take suggestions. When someone came to me with a criticism, I always assumed that it was an attempt to communicate and understand. I welcomed those encounters because it gave me valuable information that something may not be working. Fixing problems is difficult if you don't know about them. It is always much better for people to talk openly with you about issues than to talk about them behind your back. Most of the time, misunderstandings can be cleared up that would not have occurred unless someone had the courage to raise the issue. Mistakes can be acknowledged and fixed.

Everyone can learn from mistakes and this learning can strengthen an organization. However, there is a big difference between a criticism and an attack. An attack is a public denunciation that seeks to organize opposition against a leader and undermine his or her leadership.

I told many stories about attacks in the chapter on our transition years to illustrate that attacks masquerade as an attempt to correct mistakes, but the real purpose is to disrupt the smooth functioning of an organization. Attacks take attention and resources away from the real business of the organization and squander them on emotional upsets. People get confused when an attack is underway and often believe the content of the attack rather than putting their attention on the underlying causes and the effects on the organization. Leaders do not function at their best when they are under attack. A great deal of the leader's attention goes toward dealing with the attack rather than moving things forward in the organization. When an attack is underway, everyone's attention and energy gets focused on the attack rather than the real work that needs to be done. Much time and effort are wasted. The organization suffers.

Attacks need to be interrupted, preferably by those who are not the target of the attack. When a leader is being attacked, members of the organization need to step forward and demand that the attacks stop. The content of the complaint should not even be listened to until the people who are attacking agree to stop the attack. Then, a process should be set up to address the issues that need correcting.

Unfortunately, this rarely happens. An attack is usually allowed to continue with very few allies taking a stand against it. The leader is usually left to stand up for himself or herself in the face of the attack and address all the issues raised in the attack alone. This feeling of aloneness is why many leaders quit their jobs under these circumstances.

Luckily, I had many allies and was not left to handle the attacks on my own. Over the years, I got better at developing allies and letting them know how they could support me. Our board handled the last attack brilliantly and as a result, the attacks ceased. This is an excellent example of how allies can support the leader when he or she is under attack. In order to survive as a leader (with any kind of humanity intact),one must have allies around them. An ally is not someone who blindly accepts everything that a leader does; rather it is someone who will THINK about the leader. An ally will think about how to support the leader. This includes helping the leader notice and correct mistakes, as well as appreciating the hard work that the leader does. In an attack, an ally will stand with the leader and be firm against the attack. An ally will not get confused. An ally will demand that the attack stop.

Building allies is one of the most important jobs of an effective leader. Building allies involves finding people with integrity and clear thinking who can see your strengths as a leader and who will back your leadership. It is also helpful if they are clear about your weaknesses as a leader and will help and encourage you in your growth to become a better leader. Allies are people with whom you can share your thinking with and get their feedback. They are people whose thinking you can trust. I have been fortunate to have many allies who were honest enough to tell me when they thought I was off base. I appreciated their wise counsel as well as their support.

Hopefully, the stories about attacks in this book will not frighten people away from the challenges of taking on a large leadership role. Power struggles happen in any organization and my hope is that my story will help prepare leaders to recognize them for what they are early on and deal with them in a rational manner. Pleasing everyone all the time in your role as a leader is impossible. In fact, good decisions are based on thinking about what will move things forward, rather than an attempt to please everyone. This was a hard lesson for me to learn because my tendency is to want everyone to be happy all of the time. However, over time I realized that sometimes decisions had to be made that would not necessarily please everyone.

For new principals who might find themselves under attack, I would recommend the following things:

1. **Stay calm and try not to take it personally.** Most attacks masquerade as an attempt to correct a mistake, but the real purpose is to disrupt the functioning of the organization. Your attention can then go to how to best protect and move forward the

organization and its work rather than get bogged down with defending yourself. Hopefully, there will be allies to defend you so that you can keep your focus on the important work of the organization.

2. **If you have made a mistake, admit it, move quickly to fix the problem, and move on.** Don't waste time defending mistakes that you have made or feeling badly about yourself because you made a mistake. Be confident and proactive.

3. **Keep your board chair informed about all issues at the school that could become big problems.** The value of this cannot be overstated. For one, the board chair will be someone who can stand by you and help you think about the situation. Isolation as a leader should be avoided.

4. **Have good policies and procedures in place and follow them to the letter.** As a new school, we did not foresee many things. If we had had better policies and procedures, as well as a clear evaluation process for the Principal, many of the specific things that happened might have been averted.

5. **Get good advice from knowledgeable sources.** For instance, if you are dealing with a sexual harassment issue on your campus, contact the district person who deals with these issues at the district level to get ideas about how to handle it cleanly and appropriately.

6. **If you have to deal with the news media about an issue on your campus, have a clear, positive message and stick to it.**

Controlling everyone's behavior in any organization is not possible. However, people will hold you responsible for anything that happens on campus. There is always the chance that something dreadful can happen that is beyond your control. Time after time, we have all witnessed that when something bad happens in government, sports, education, whatever, the leader is fired whether or not he or she had any contact with the situation. People are always looking for someone to blame.

You can't waste your time worrying about this. You just have to do your best to create a safe environment, have good policies and procedures in place, hire good people, and hold up high expectations for everyone's conduct. Even when you do that vigilantly, things can happen.

One thing that I noticed in my role as principal was that I no longer got frightened as easily. When you survive hard times, you realize how strong you are. Every situation that challenged me required that I kept thinking clearly and moving things forward. Being confronted with challenges that are uncomfortable is what causes a leader to grow. There is no growth without struggle.

My Views on the Charter School Movement

I am proud of the charter school movement and what we have accomplished in a short period of time. The variety of educational options that are now available to parents for their children is truly remarkable. However, some supporters of charter schools act as though all charter schools are good and district-run public schools are not. I believe that there are good and bad district schools as well as good and bad charter schools, and there are certain ingredients that make a school great regardless of its structure.

Those on both sides who work to create an adversarial position between charter schools and district schools are putting their own personal agendas ahead of the best interests of students. There are as many different types of school districts as there are charter schools. Many districts, like the one where my charter school is located, have leadership that is proactive, forward thinking, and put kids first. Their schools are some of the best in the state. There are other districts that are still living in the past with no vision for the future, failing to meet the needs of their students, threatened by new ideas, and of course, there is everything in between these two extremes.

There are some charter schools where students excel in innovative programs that empower teachers and parents and are managed in a fiscally sound manner. On the other hand, there are also charter schools that are run by for-profit management companies that have the capital to start a myriad of "cookie cutter schools" offering nothing unique and paying their teachers minimally with mediocre results in order to make a profit for the company. And there is everything in between these two extremes. We need to be supporting all good schools and changing (or closing) the ones that are failing whether they are charter or not.

I am a big supporter of charter schools because I believe in educators and parents being empowered to start the school of their dreams. However, I do not support all charter schools, especially if they are centrally controlled with "shadow boards" that exist in name only or schools who mismanage their finances or schools where students are not improving in their performance. Believe me, while sitting on the Florida Charter School Appeals Commission, I saw all kinds.

We will not change education if we continue to have an "us" versus "them" mindset. We need to be saying, "Does this school work or not?" Districts and charter schools can work together by putting students first. I know this because my charter school and our district have had an excellent relationship. We offer something that the district doesn't have and our students excel in our program. We strengthen our district and they are proud that we exist. As a result, they do much to help us.

Some charter school operators in Florida complain about the 5 percent of the state funds that districts charge charter schools for services. I have never complained about this because we have received our money's worth of resources from the district. However, supporters of charter schools in the Florida Legislature changed this rule in that charter schools only pay the district 5 percent of its revenue for the first 250 students. This ruling unfairly favors the large charter schools and reduces the amount of services that the district is willing to provide. Our school, with 270 students, pays about the same amount as we always did to the district while large charter schools pay much less, but we suffer disproportionately by the reduction of services. Sometimes in an attempt to help charter schools, a law can inadvertently harm the smaller ones while helping the larger ones.

Another issue that divides people concerning charter schools is teacher unions. Teacher unions don't like charter schools because charter schools are not unionized. Likewise, others gleefully support charter schools because there are no teacher unions. While I can understand both of these viewpoints, I think that the most important point is missed in this debate: teachers are the heroes and heroines of society. They should be adequately compensated for their work which is some of the most important work in the world. That's the bottom line. The teacher unions have fought for this principle for decades and they are right. This society does not sufficiently support education and teachers are not adequately paid. I will always stand behind this noble cause that is still being fought by the teacher unions.

Unions in this country have historically fought to protect workers and have insisted on the passage of laws that are important to our society, such as the 40-hour work week and child labor laws. These laws have humanized our society by raising living standards and have pushed against the notion that profits are more important than people. We sometimes hear about horrible working conditions in other countries, but this is how our own factories used to be before labor unions organized for better working conditions. Unions serve an important role in making sure that the people who provide the labor are not forgotten in the constant rush for profits. In a nation where income inequality has been growing since the 1970s, labor unions are needed as a hedge against this trend. However, those who would rather return to the era of unregulated capitalism have demonized labor unions.

Even though I am a charter school leader, I am not anti-union. Unions have been in my family for generations. My great grandparents homesteaded in North Dakota and my grandmother sang Farmer's Union songs to me as a child. In order to survive, Midwestern farmers had to unite against the big banks and railroads that were squeezing them during the first half of the 1900s. My father was a teacher in Pensacola after retiring from the US Navy. He participated in the last teacher strike in the state of Florida in 1968. I was in high school at the time and attended meetings with him during the strike while the schools were closed. I listened to many speeches and understood the reasons behind the strike. I even wrote a letter to the editor of the local newspaper, the Pensacola News Journal, supporting the teachers. After college, when I entered the teaching profession, I joined the local teacher union and was a member of the National Education Association (NEA). I have always supported teachers and their struggle to be adequately compensated for the hard work that they do. I have always valued the contributions of NEA in furthering education and other important issues in our country.

However, once I started leading a charter school, I came to understand the value of annual contracts in the pursuit of the best school possible. Many school districts have found it difficult to remove a poor teacher from the classroom after they get tenure. In a charter school, everyone serves "at will" and is not necessarily rehired at the end of a school year. Because of this, a charter school can keep improving the teaching staff every year. Schools are not assembly lines and teaching is different from a job in a factory. Teachers work with young, impressionable minds every day and the experiences that these young people have in schools affects them throughout their lives. Being a good teacher requires more than knowledge and skill; it requires a certain temperament and ability to reach young people. It is not a job that everyone can do.

To keep an inadequate teacher in the classroom does a huge disservice to the students who have to be in that teacher's classroom. For this reason, I support annual contracts for teachers. Being a good teacher is an extremely difficult and time-consuming job. This should be recognized as such with high standards of accountability and adequate pay. Those who do not meet those high standards should find other employment that better suits their talents. The students should come first.

I need to point out that some charter schools pay incredibly low wages to teachers in order to turn a profit for the management company. This is just plain wrong. Education for profit has no place in the public educational system and should not be allowed. All taxpayer dollars going toward education ought to go to the children not be siphoned off as profits for a management company. Restrictions should be placed on the ways that some management companies hide their profits in the budget, such as through large lease payments on school buildings. At our school, we attempt to pay our lead teachers near that which was agreed upon through the district's collective bargaining process. We don't always achieve that level for a variety of financial reasons, but that is the goal for which we strive. We don't do this because we are required to, but because we want to attract the best teachers and pay them what the local area has determined is appropriate. Charter schools should work hard to compensate teachers adequately, as well as treat them respectfully and give them a voice in running the school. Teachers should avoid working at any school that does not value them and does not understand that a good teaching staff is the key to having a good school.

Charter schools are held to high standards of accountability in regards to student achievement and rightly so. Charter schools with low student achievement are often closed because they have not shown that their program is successful. The debate over standardized testing is going strong inside and outside the charter school world and for good reason. While we need data to determine whether students are successful or not, education that is boiled down to a test score is lacking in some of the key ingredients that define an educated and well-rounded person. As a colleague of mine on the Task Force for Charter School Quality and Accountability noted, "A good school will have good test scores. However, just because a school has high test scores does not automatically make it a good school." A school can become so focused on test scores that all resources are placed on math, reading, and science to the exclusion of the arts and the social studies. Demonstration of excellence in the arts cannot be reduced to a test score. Performance is the key. Thankfully, the state assessment doesn't include a section for social studies or that subject matter would be reduced to rote memory rather than critical thinking, analysis, debate, discussion, and presentation which are better ways to demonstrate competency in this area. A good school is one where students develop skills for participating collaboratively in a democratic society rather than just memorizing a bunch of facts or equations. A good school will have good test scores and much, much more.

Many have pointed out that test scores are actually a socioeconomic score. The gap in test scores between rich and poor children is 30-40 percent wider than it was 25 years ago. Schools that serve affluent neighborhoods tend to have much higher scores than those that don't. There are many reasons for this and no one can disagree that poverty, racism, and the hopelessness that comes with it take a huge toll on the ability of many young people to focus on learning. However, there are many charter school heroes, like Dr. Deborah Kenny of Harlem Village Academies, who have opened schools that serve low income neighborhoods and they have created cultures where the goal is success. I have visited successful inner-city charter high schools around the country where the goal has been that every student will graduate and go to college. Some districts have accomplished this too, but there is nothing like the passion of a fired-up, mission-driven school to overcome the odds. These schools are models of success and their methods should be researched and replicated everywhere.

Charter schools are businesses. Just like in the business world, there are "Mom and Pop" stores and there are large corporations. Competition is tough and the rules favor the large businesses. In addition, economies of scale play a role. If you are a person like me who thinks that smaller schools are better able to create a respectful learning environment that is more human because people can be more connected with each other, then the trick is to find the right size to remain economically viable. You need to be just big enough to be able to survive financially, but not so big that you lose touch with the people who you serve—the students. You need to be big enough to have the resources to offer a full range of opportunities and courses and pay your teachers competitively while maintaining a "family atmosphere" on campus where everyone knows each other and no one gets lost in the masses. This is not easy to do, especially when funds for public education keep coming under the knife. As the economic situation in society has worsened, our school has had to grow to survive. However, we remain as small as we can for the good of our students.

I noticed when I was on the Florida Charter School Appeals Commission that it was much easier for a large school or one represented by a management company to win their appeal—or even to find the resources to appeal at all. When you can pay for attorneys to represent you and professionals to write your application, you have a better chance. I am not advocating lowering the standards, but just like in the larger economy, I encourage decision-makers to find ways to encourage and support the "Mom and Pops." They are the essence of the charter school movement. Those grassroots parents and teachers who want to start the school of their dreams should have our respect and support because it is often from those places where the fresh thinking and new solutions come. Likewise, it is usually those schools where the parents and teachers are the most empowered.

Charter schools must meet high standards of accountability for student achievement, financial responsibility, and innovation. This is important for the students and it is important for the charter school movement. Failing charter schools that are allowed to continue only hurt the image of charter schools everywhere. These are the schools that usually get coverage on the front pages of newspapers. This is not good for anyone. Districts and other authorizers must have the courage to shut down low performing charter schools. When I served on the Florida Charter School Appeals Commission, we upheld the terminations of low performing charter schools every time.

In the early days of the charter school movement, in order to get the legislation to start this grand experiment, charter school leaders said that we could do a better job with fewer resources than district-run public education. The result is a system where charter schools receive fewer public resources than district schools. Once we started operating charter schools and understood the reality of what it takes, the unfairness of this situation became obvious. Parents have asked, "Why should my child receive fewer resources just because he or she goes to a charter school?" One of the biggest issues for the charter school movement is equity in funding. The way to solve this problem is legislation that grants this equality. As a result, charter schools (as public schools) would receive their fair share of the tax dollars collected through federal, state, and local taxes.

Sometimes I long for the early days when charter schools were new. In those days, we had so much more freedom to try new things and truly innovate. The promise was that charter schools would deliver better results in return for greater freedom. Over the years, so many new regulations have been added by state legislatures that it has formed a straitjacket around innovative schools that have to conform to all kinds of rigid rules. The myriad rules and procedures that are now required are burdensome and overwhelming to the small management teams in small charter schools. I understand that these regulations were necessitated by some who took advantage of the leniency in those early days and did a poor job of managing their schools, but for those of us who worked hard to be innovative while successfully managing our schools and producing excellent academic results, the shift toward more regimentation with less flexibility is disappointing. My question is: why go to all of the bother to start a school if you can't reach for something more innovative than has ever been conceived?

One of the pleasures of being involved in the charter school movement is the diversity of ideas and theories about how best to educate children. The charter school movement is a big tent—a very big tent. Although we share a passion for the charter schools that we have created, we represent many different perspectives on every issue. Because of this, many charter school people will disagree with some of the views that I have presented here. One of the strengths of the charter school movement is that it has brought together people from different political parties, ideologies, and philosophies of education with the common goal of offering choices for parents, students, and teachers. Choice is one of the most important advantages of living in a great democracy like ours. School choice is the cornerstone of the charter school movement.

Epilogue

It is good to report that the School of Arts and Sciences continues to do well in my absence. The school has held true to its philosophical foundations while students and teachers thrive in a respectful, joyous learning environment. The school continues to be a high performing school by every measure, including student test scores. Every year when the local paper presents the top high school graduates in the city, a notable percentage were former students at our school. In addition, the board and staff are working hard to expand the school and eventually to replicate it. They have recently purchased property adjoining the school and have expanded the student population. There are plans for a new building in the future.

There are two dangers facing the school. One is that it must grow in order to survive financially with its outstanding academic program intact. Keeping the small school advantages as they grow bigger will be a challenge. Also, financing facilities remains the biggest hurdle for small charter schools. However, I have no doubt that they will solve this problem. The bigger danger to the school is "creeping traditionalism." Implementing a traditional curriculum is easier than striving continuously for innovation and fresh ideas. To stay on course requires commitment and attention. Sometimes the people who are the most passionate about innovation--move on and are replaced with others who may not have the same vision. The danger over time is burnout and a return to an easier way of doing things. On top of this is the pressure from the state legislature to standardize and bureaucratize everything more and more. It will take heroic efforts on the part of all future boards and principals to keep this school on track and not lose sight of the vision. My hope is that the vision can be passed on and will persist.

When I contemplated leaving the school, I wondered who I would be without the school. For more than a decade, my identity had been tied up in my role as principal and I wondered who I would be without that role. I should not have worried. My life has unfolded in a wonderful way. It is a joyous experience to recreate your life and dream new dreams. I am living my dream in the Montana wilderness for six months each year and return to Tallahassee to my camellias, citrus trees, and dancing for the other six months. I am happier than I ever thought possible.

While the first draft of this book was the easiest because the writing just flowed out of me, subsequent drafts were more difficult to write as I fine-tuned my memories by reading archived school documents. I also met with a number of groups and individuals to listen to their stories and see the school's history through their eyes.

I do my best writing on rainy days. After spending my career inside a building focused on the business of education, I cannot tolerate being inside when the weather is lovely outside. My new lifestyle split between Florida (November-April) and Montana (May-October) has provided me with two springs (March and April are spring in Tallahassee while May and June are spring in Montana) and two falls (September and October are fall in Montana while November and December are fall in Tallahassee) along with great outdoor weather in both summer and winter. Because I like to be outside, this book has taken me longer to write than I had planned. Despite my reluctance at times, I had a commitment to myself to finish it.

I wrote this book because I thought that the story of the School of Arts and Sciences should be told. My hope is that others will realize that it is possible to create the school of your dreams.

Acknowledgements

There were many people who helped me with this book. I am particularly grateful to Patti Craig-Hart who made many edits and suggestions on every page of the first draft. She did this again after I completed the fifth draft. It is a better book because of her careful eye for detail. Betsy Holycross offered important suggestions that re-energized me and encouraged me to write a fifth draft when I was ready to throw my hands up in frustration. Basically, she told me to "take off my rose-colored glasses and tell the real story of what really happened" including all of the struggles and feelings of doubt. Others who read various drafts and offered comments were Diane Shisk, Sharon Kant-Rauch, Lyn Kittle, Anthony Gaudio, Iris Palazesi, Terry Kant-Rauch, Julie Fredrickson, Bill Fordyce, and Cathryn Lokey. In addition to this help, various groups met with me to remember stories from the early years. Some of those people were Anne Meisenzahl, Roger Peace, Roger Pinholster, Julie Fredrickson, Mary DeHoff, Lyn Kittle, and Anthony Gaudio. Additional help on details came from Bev Owens and Kristen Craig. Many co-counselors listened to me as I thought through various details. Finally, Amelie Dawson professionally edited the entire book before it was published. Her copy editing and suggestions for changes helped me polish the final draft.

Although a large number of people contributed to the vision in the original charter application, I would like to thank the people who were listed as the founders of the school: Dr. Carolyn Schluck, Dr. Mary Markin, Dr. Roger Pinholster, Dr. Gerald Schluck, and Maureen Yoder. Their vision and persistence began the dream.

I would also like to thank all of the people who served as board chair during my tenure as principal: Dr. Mary Markin, Dr. Roger Pinholster, Terry Kant-Rauch, Lyn Kittle, Joy Moore, Anthony Gaudio, Susan Parks, and Dr. Iris Palazesi. Their strong, inspired leadership helped guide the school through many challenges and successes. They contributed their clear thinking, passion and energy, and countless volunteer hours to making the school a success. In addition, I thank Dr. Jim Croteau, Bev Owens, and Jackie Pons from Leon County Schools, along with the Leon County School Board, for their support over the years.

Some of the biggest heroes of the school are those parents who volunteered their time, energy, and commitment over the entire history of the school and took on whatever tasks the school needed at the time. Although there were many parents who volunteered countless hours to the school, a couple of them went way beyond the call of duty. You won't find their names on a building, but we would not have had such an excellent school had it not been for their dedication to it.

One parent in particular exemplified the dedication of our parents and contributed to the success of our school for the entire time that I was the principal. Lyn Kittle found a variety of niches in which to contribute to the school in all of its various phases. She was the parent liaison to the board during the period prior to the school's opening when the principal and business manager were hired. During our early years, she volunteered countless hours running the admissions process, managing the website, and keeping parents informed through e-mail. She became a member of the board of directors and served as the chair for two years. Lyn was an amazing ally for me during hard times and attacks on my leadership. She was a superb editor and gave me feedback on many documents that I wrote. She worked with the parent organization and served on the school advisory council. During my last years at the school, Lyn was hired as the office manager. She did all of the jobs that the front office person does and she handled it all in the most professional and organized way; however, I do not believe that we utilized her skills in the best way possible. She was so talented and knowledgeable about the school that she should have been my administrative assistant (had we been able to afford such a position) rather than a glorified receptionist in the front office. The school owes her a tremendous debt of gratitude for all of the behind-the-scenes work that she did for thirteen years.

Another parent who worked tirelessly for the school was Anthony Gaudio. As a volunteer, Anthony used his expertise in the building trades to oversee many facility projects. He used the machinery from his business for excavating and earthmoving in order to solve our flooding problems. He was our liaison with the construction manager during the creation of our new building and helped to solve some issues with the building after it was built. He served on the board of directors and was the chair during some of the most tumultuous years of the school, including the lawsuit against the board. As a board member, he chaired the finance committee and was instrumental in arranging the financing for the new building and some property that we wanted to purchase. He was always talking about the school to leaders in the wider community in order to recruit experienced people for the board of directors. Later, we hired him as our financial services person to handle the school's finances and accounting. He was someone who I could always count on.

About the Author..........

After teaching for 21 years, "Principal Powers" helped open the School of Arts and Sciences in 1999 as the founding principal. In just five years, the school was named one of the top eight charter schools in the nation for innovation and accountability by the US Department of Education. A short time later, it was named a model school among all types of schools in the nation by the International Center for Leadership in Education. While principal, Debo served on the National Task Force for Charter School Quality and Accountability, the Florida Charter School Review Panel, the Florida Charter School Appeals Commission, and the Advocacy Committee for the Florida Consortium of Charter Schools. Numerous times, she has spoken to education committees in the Florida Legislature. She served as principal for thirteen years before retiring. She continues to lead the half-day principal's networking session at the annual Florida Charter School Conference and to serve on the Charter School Appeals Commission when she is needed. She writes a monthly blog for charter school principals called "Leading the Dream."

Not only is Debo a charter school leader, but she is a dance competitor and instructor, a regional leader in Re-evaluation Counseling, certified camellia show judge, and an environmental activist. She built a solar-powered cabin in the Montana wilderness next to Glacier National Park where she lives off-the-grid and loves to hike, backpack, kayak, mountain bike, and garden. She took her ideas about working collaboratively into her Montana community and served as President of the North Fork Landowners Association with a focus on community building. She also served on the Whitefish Range Partnership, a collaborative effort that brought together loggers, snowmobilers, mountain bikers, backcountry horsemen, hikers, hunters, anglers, and wilderness advocates to reach consensus on a recommendation for land management in the Flathead National Forest in Montana. She currently serves on the board of several environmental organizations in Montana and donates her time as a volunteer fire lookout during fire season. In her retirement, she splits her time between Montana and Florida.